ACKNOWLEDGMENTS

My zeal of writing this book has been to raise awareness for all the girls on this side of the world, who have it so well, but are still unsatisfied and unhappy; To help them appreciate their parents to whom they owe their life. I would not have made it without the help of my friends to whom I am immensely grateful. My special thanks are directed to Beverly Trainer, Editor, for all the time and care she generously invested in guiding me to put the idea together.

To my good friend Bryan Kistler for his time, reading and correcting the book with care, interest, and enthusiasm, so I can successfully put into words, what I had in mind.

More over to my good friends, Peggi Braams-and especially-Nancy Kister, for their the moral support. Nancy has always been there, when I needed her.

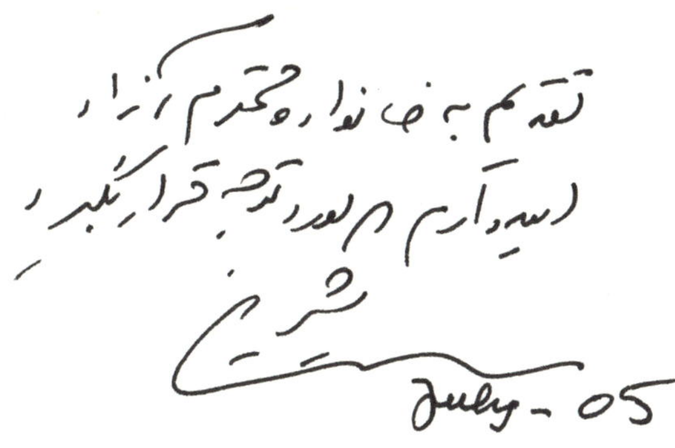

FREEDOM:
OVER THE OCEANS,
OTHER SIDE OF THE MOUNTAINS

An Emotional True Story of a Courageous Iranian Woman

By
Shirin Brown

PublishAmerica
Baltimore

First printing

ISBN: 1-4137-2303-9
PUBLISHED BY PUBLISHAMERICA, LLLP
www.publishamerica.com
Baltimore

Printed in the United States of America

In the memory of my parents who taught me the art of survival, each in their own way.

With love to my two children, who are my only reasons to live. And to my husband for his devotion to my children.

..o..TABLE OF CONTENTS..o..

PART I
THE END

CHAPTER 1
The Storyteller

It's one in the morning. I'm still wide-awake, sitting at my desk and looking out the window. I can't see much outside. Wherever the moon is, it is not at our side. Many hours lie ahead until daylight. I turn on the computer and try to put my thoughts into words. I write:

> *There comes a time in life when we cannot deny the trace of aging in us. A time when we do not even try to deny. There comes a time when the days shrink, the nights prolong. And the clock gets stuck through restless nights.*
>
> *There comes a time when our value grades change. What remains is not a big dream, or the wish to have or to hold. It is time to let go of what's gone, time to forgive and forget, and for withdrawal. Over those long, bungling years when days delay and nights seem to be there to stay, all we can do to push through is to reminisce and review; to think and appraise the past.*

There, I stop writing; *it is my turn now,* I think to myself. I have a lot to recall, much to think about, until the rims of the next dawn glow, and let me know that the night's withdrawn and another day is born. I turn off the lights. The computer screen looks shinier. Not everything looks like reality in the dark. It is staring at me like the one-eyed dragon. It doesn't frighten me, though. Nothing scares me anymore.

Sitting still, looking at the gray screen, my thoughts start to fly.

Every blink of the cursor takes me farther ... and farther... far beyond the here and now.

Then the cursor disappears. The screen starts to spin, spiral like, creeping towards me. I feel weightless, floating through the murky haze that fills the room. I glide deep and deeper, as far as my memories allow. There, I see something familiar. A shape similar to the profile of a seated cat. It's head is upright, looking at me. I glide closer. Yes, I recognize what it is. It's my home. My country...Persia. Better known as Iran today.

"The map of Persia looks just like a sitting cat," the history teacher used to say. I still remember. God knows how many times we practiced to draw that map correctly at school. The outline of that familiar piece of earth we belonged to.

In the dim light of my bedroom it echoes, the melody of a song. Music is a part of my soul, and I have listened to this one so often. It is called "The Green Grass of Home." I know all the words:

".... The old home-town looks the same,
as I step down from the train,
and there to meet me, is my mama and papa...
Down the road I look, and there runs Mary,
hair gold and lips like cherries, its good to touch
The green, green grass of home. . .."

Just below the arm of the sitting cat, I see a sparkling star. That is where I lived – Teheran – today's capital city of Iran. Further down, I see another one shining – Esfahan. There, in a silver bowl of light I see Mother lying in bed screaming. A new beginning, a baby girl is being born. It is the first of four children, three girls in three years and, five years later, a boy, her favorite. "I would have gone on to bear children, until I had a boy." She always mentioned jokingly. Yet, on the serious note, it was the norm at those times and the place.

It comes to me what some believe, that the creation started with an explosion in the emptiness. And the part assigned to us to live on was the Earth, as we call it. You see, it appears that the kind of life we get to live is pre-determined by the place and the time we are born. If in the East, West, North, or the South of the planet, during a time of war or peace. So is our skin color, if red or white, black or yellow. But have "we" been selected just by random? Do we play any part in all this?

I return to this family of six. The story is about the first-born girl, whom I know too well. The time is right. It is 1946, one year after a joyous ending. The Second World War. A few years before that, life would have been different in Persia and almost everywhere in the world. But the place? Well, most of her life she was in the wrong place. It took her forty-odd years to find the right one.

I see that place and hear the melody going on in my head. I whisper along:

"The old house is still standing...
though the paint is cracked and dry.
And that's the old old tree that I used to play on,
down the lane I walk with my sweet Mary
hair gold and lips like cherries its good
To touch the green green grass of home...."

I remember my mother always said: "Don't go too far in search for the meaning of life, it can drive you crazy." How right she was. Now that I have all the time in the world to think about it, I do not. Since I have decided that it is all for "the mission" that we have come to this world to accomplish. And our destiny drives us towards the fulfillment of that "goal." I now believe, what we get out of life is what we put into it. And all that happens to us is what we do to ourselves. In the running, still, not always do we realize if we are on the right track. We might sometime, near to the end, just too late for regrets or detours. And all those who could have steered us between the lines, are long gone.

Soon I'll hear the early birds singing. I have done this so often. I turn the light on. The music is gone. For now, it is just me, and the deadly silence of the night. So, I start writing again. About all what "was," and turned to enlarged photographs on the walls; to some letters and sealed papers in a binder, and a few precious little objects.

Tonight I let the music play, and memories tell the tale. It is time for the pictures on the wall to talk. The dry roses on the bookcase, and the small size wedding ring, to sing. The carefully hidden somewhere, I forgot, one half of a "paper money" to remind me of the sweetest part of my past. And I wonder *where is he now?* The one who has the other half. The one from whom I learned, for a very short time, what love truly was. Thinking of him still makes me hear my heartbeat. And I can touch and feel the green grass of home. The song goes on:

"Then I wake and look around me,
at the four gray walls that surround me,
And I realize, yes, I was only dreaming."

Nineteen years go by in a blink of an eye, as I see her again. The first-born. The little curly hair, happy baby has now grown up to a good-looking young girl. She has long brown hair and bright brown eyes. But this is not the same happy soul that she was.

Some say: "A happy childhood promises a happy life." *Does it really?* I ask myself.

As I was watching the screen turned black. It got dark. It was late at night, maybe even one in the morning. And this is when it all began, and what I saw.

CHAPTER 2
In Iran

She was only nineteen. And that night was the night before her wedding day. A small ceremony to be held in the absence of the groom. The groom was in Germany at the time, so his father would say, "I do" on his behalf. It was the last night that she was spending in her parents' home. Traditionally in Iran, girls would live with their parents until they get married.

On that remarkable night of every girl's life, she was lonely and sad. She had nobody to talk to but her little red diary book. She opened the first page. It was dated three years back. The day she first noticed her future husband. Disappointed but calm, she turned to the last page and wrote:

> *I wish these past pages didn't exist. They tell me how I have been wasting my life. I know we are not right for each other. I know I am making a big mistake marrying him. Well, if I don't, I'll be doomed and, my family's good name destroyed. It is insane, ha? You know well how it works in our society. What I have done, for the last three years, having a "boy-friend" is a Sin. That is why I am forcing myself into this marriage. I am only trying to clean up my mess; this ugly grave wound, which I have brought on my family's name. Besides, no other man would take me after all this. He is bad, I can change him.*
>
> *The new chapter of my life begins tomorrow with a hallowed ceremony. I didn't want any of it at all, but Mom insisted, "What*

would people think? We have to do something!" She said. "I'll pay for it if his parents don't." Well they didn't, although traditionally it was their duty. I didn't want Mom to pay for anything! But she did it anyway. To me, it felt as if she was spending her money to get rid of me.

Well, my dearest friend and confidant, you have been listening to my confessions patiently, so generously all this time. Stories of my joys and sorrows, heartaches and blessings. It has been a great relief talking to you. But I guess this is the last time we talk. We have to part now. And I have no more space left to write, so it is time to say good-by. Please wish me luck.

Her sister was in deep sleep in the bed near hers. She closed her diary, staring at its red cover for a long while as her childhood and teen years drifted away, disappearing in the past. A few teardrops rolled down her cheeks and dropped on the book. The wet spots on the red cover of her diary brought her back to where she was. She carefully wiped them off, and put her closest friend back in its hiding place.

Trapped and isolated in a cage designed by her chastity, she could see no way out. She feared the future. It was cold, and in the loneliness of her bedroom, the world was turning upside-down. So, she gently crawled under the blanket, and hugged her knees, pressing them hard against her chest, in an effort to feel safe. Yet, a storm of self-doubts and unasked questions in her head were keeping her up.

The scenes of tomorrow's events came to life in front of her eyes. The whole family was there; it was loud music in their house where the ceremony was being held. But that was the only traditional part. The rest was not there. She was not wearing a proper wedding gown, just an ordinary short white dress. And although it was a white wedding, no white lace veiled her face or head.

She saw her father; he looked dazed and was quiet. Her mother, she was pretending to be happy. And there was a picture of the groom on a chair.

What a humiliation, she thought. But for now, there was only silence, the wet pillow of her tears, and her hopeless cries numbed within her. Thoughts and buried words were running through her mind:

Mom, do you remember after he left for Germany, I got seriously ill? And the family physician told you that I was lovesick? How wrong he was, Mom. I shouldn't have trusted him with my secret. I wasn't lovesick. I was ruined. Because he left to put me under pressure to join him. At that point, I wished I could end my relationship. But then, how would I explain it to you and everyone. I was terrified.

Mom, at that most desperate time of my life, I needed you more than ever. I wished I could run to you, put my head on your lap, just like the old times when I was a little girl; so you rub my back and play with the curls of my hair. But you distanced yourself from me. I had hurt you, and jeopardized your place in society -- The society that is now burying me alive. You didn't have the courage to listen to me; to tell me that I was jumping to conclusions. So, my innocent secrets, which I did not dare to talk about to anyone, went lost in my diary.

You believed the physician, and overlooked the signs of confusion in the face of your puzzled teenager. And I had to hide myself like a dying, ill animal.

Mom, there were times that I even wished you'd have faced me, punished me and told me that I was wrong. About everything; "you, me, us."

She took a deep breath trying to re-experience the tranquilizing scent of her mother's body. It was hard, for it went back too long, but it still was soothing, and relaxed her.

The night was growing old, and the steady sound of raindrops, falling on the plane trees in the dark and soaked little side-yard behind the window of her bedroom, put her to sleep.

PART II
SHATTERED IN GERMANY

CHAPTER 3
The Wedding Night

She endured the ceremony bravely. Six months later, she was on a flight to Germany to join her husband. But that flight turned into the beginning of a long journey, holding the most unusual, unexpected chain of events. The events, which determined the way she was to go for many years to come. Like one domino nudging the next, they drew her down for the rest of her life.

A journey over which she found herself being pushed and pulled by the crowd. Getting squeezed and squashed, like an abandoned canoe on the edge of Niagara Falls, crashing down unwittingly. Only to get up and start over again, gathering her scattered broken pieces before they were rushed away along the river flow.

When the shiny, metallic iron bird, a 707, broke through the ocean of high clouds, the sun started to shine again. She lay back in her seat and accepted the cold drink offered by a very friendly flight attendant, not knowing that it was the last friendly face she would come across for a long time.

With her was her father, a calm, quiet, loving man. She was convinced that he too was not glad about this marriage, but for some strange reason he made no attempt to stop her. *Maybe he lost the fight against Mom,* she thought. He was snoring away, and missed the drinks.

She settled into her cozy corner, sipped her drink, and let loose with the rush of her uncontrolled thoughts. There was a plain big screen ahead of her, leaving behind everything she had and who she was. It all began to roll in front of her eyes like a silent movie.

She saw herself at home, a cheerful and lively girl of six. One by one the early mornings' adventures with her younger sister Shana. The days that Mother woke them before dawn, and sent them out for a ride on their tricycles to enjoy the sunrise, unfolding in the back of the old parliament building not far from their house.

Then she saw the far end of the garden and the beautiful tall and colorful cherry tree, which they used to play under. She was there, her two sisters, and their three cousins, picking the cherries before the birds ate them all. And like most of the times, there was also her shy childhood sweetheart, who never admitted how much she meant to him at the time. He always insisted on playing "her" husband in their group. And soon disappeared when she lost her head about that "handsome boy on the bus."

Every little thing was so clear, so shiny and real: the view of the Damavand mountains from the small balcony of the house which overlooked the narrow asphalt road where they used to ride their bikes, chased by the neighborhood boys.

The shine of the white marble front of the house where she grew into a lively teenager. And the good-looking face of the grocer in his small shop at the end of the road, where they always found something to buy!

There, she heard it again. The voice of the funny old man who carried melons for sale, over-loaded on his aged donkey. He used to make his own passionate songs about the quality of his melons. And they always heard him singing them, long before they saw him walking proudly up the road. There was no place left for him to sit on the animal, so he walked along with his donkey. They seemed happy together, like good friends.

And then, the cheeky face of the nice young mailman who secretly handed her over the letters from Germany through the little restroom window that opened to the side road.

A sudden jolt of the plane made it all disappear. She looked out the window. It was dark, and all she could see was the wing of the aircraft. Passengers were watching a movie; her father, squashed in his seat, was still asleep.

She turned to the window, looking through the black veil of darkness at the vacuum behind the thick plastic; she asked herself, *am I going to miss it all? The squeaky winter noise of the worn wheels of the old wooden pushcart, rolling strenuously on the asphalt, as the short, fat, and wrinkle-faced oil-shop owner pushed it grudgingly down the road, delivering burn-oil for the heaters? Or that cold and snowy winter day when we slid down the icy road, all the way to school? Am I ever going to see my old school again?*

She could remember so vividly: The very last time at school, it was one week after graduation. She needed to be there once more. It was one of those hot summer days when their high heels sank into the asphalt. The school was frightfully quiet and empty when she arrived.

Heavy-hearted, she walked into each classroom, touching the desks as she passed them. She could hear the noise; see her friends, herself, and the intense, happy years they had spent there together.

Where did they all go? She asked herself.

That day she paused by each and every object, trying to etch all the details in her memory. She was taking deep breaths all along, to inhale as much as she could of that intimate scent of the classroom. That dear familiar scent, a mixture of chalk, wood, and thick air, imprisoned between the four white walls and the closed windows. She was trying to take with her a small part of the most treasured period of her life, dissolved in her bloodstream.

Why do I have a feeling that I am going to lose all this? She wondered as she finally left the school for the very last time, carrying the burden of an endless sorrow on her fallen shoulders. The sorrow of her first experience of the end. A period of life that was concluded and gone, never to return. "intense," as the painful feeling of grief.

She remembered that it all started there, when she was sixteen. The first time she noticed this handsome boy, watching her, she was in the bus, coming home from school. He was handsome, tall, and sporty, about her age. She didn't think much of him. To her he was yet another good looking, rude school-boy in the bus. But time proved otherwise as he continued stalking her, for days and weeks, and then months.

He timed his traveling every day so that he caught the same public bus at the same time she did. Just to be near her. It was not unusual in the Teheran of those years. Teenage boys did that. It was their way to attract girls' attention and hopefully get a date. But, as "good girls" did not date easily, it sometimes turned into a long process, requiring much effort and patience.

A whole year passed and he didn't miss a day. And then another year went by. He had become a permanent part of her days, growing more daring. Telling her he loved her, asking her for a date, loud and clear, so that everyone in the bus would turn around and look at her in strange way. Standing all the way in walkway of the bus, by her seat, talking to her despite the empty seats he could take.

She ignored him all the way. But his persistence had begun to stir her. She was beginning to notice changes in her feelings for him. Her heart pounded against her chest when she saw him, and pumped an unknown warmth and gentle feeling through her veins. They were inexplicable, pleasant, and sometimes painful feelings. It was getting harder and harder for her to deny. Yet she did, until that day.

The graduation year was coming to an end, and soon everyone would go their separate ways. That day, he approached her spontaneously as he stepped into the bus. He took her by the arms and looked straight into her eyes. "Hey, tell me, is your heart made of bricks? I love you, and I know that you love me too. I want an answer. If you don't call me by the end of this week, you'll never see me again, so give me a call," he said and jumped off the bus at the very next stop.

That afternoon she lived through a nightmare. She panicked. His warning had made her stand face-to-face with her hidden feelings. She suddenly realized that she didn't want to lose him. She was getting used to him. To hear him say, "I love you," and begging her for a date. She was secretly expecting him.

That evening she waited for the dark to take over, and her sister to go to sleep. Then she seized her only confidant, and wrote:

> *...What should I do? How can I date him? My parents, both highly respected physicians, are too strict with us. We are not even allowed to go out with the girls. In this country where the girls and boys go to separate schools, what would people think? Me, with a "boy friend"? They'll kill me.*
>
> *But what if "he" gives up? What if he doesn't appear tomorrow? I am going to die if I don't see him any more. Do you think I am falling in love?*

Her longing for love was pushing her to break the golden cage and fly out. But she had to choose. Between her desire and her virtue. The choice she had to make turned into a bitter struggle the rest of the week. It left her lost and lonely, while "he" didn't show up anymore.

Finally, at the end of that week on a dreamy spring Friday, as the sun was preparing to move away and the sky blue turned into red and orange, she lost the battle and picked the phone up. It was the very first time she was talking to him. She was trembling, feeling hot and heavy. She couldn't remember what she said or heard. When she put the phone down, she was upset for her weakness, but relieved; feeling exhausted, yet released.

Soon they were dating secretly. She was entering a completely new world. In his arms, she found warmth, attention, and the feeling of being needed. His passion took her high above the earth. She traveled over the clouds with him, through the cool breeze, under never-ending full moons. In a short while, she felt so secure that she no longer worried about her parents, or the future without him. Nothing could stop her now, and the way back was long closed.

Time went by, fast, while she lived in her dream world. Until the time when she reached the moment of reality, and fell straight down to the earth. After graduation, he decided to take a two-year scholarship for an engineering course in Germany. He suggested they go to Germany together.

"To do that we have to get married first." She mentioned cautiously.

"Then you'd better tell your mother about our plans. I can't afford getting married." He answered abruptly.

"I don't want a big wedding," she pleaded. "As long as it makes it legal for me to travel with you."

He shrugged his shoulders, "Big or small, I don't have money to do anything, and don't forget the money I will receive would not be enough for two people to live on. Therefore your parents have to pay for your traveling expenses and your living expenses for the two years."

The earth quivered under her feet. She wished it would open and let her sink in. But, she knew she *had* to marry him now, or else he would be gone.

His response to her "proposal" shocked her. She had never dreamed of a spectacular wedding, but going with him unmarried was unthinkable, and he knew it. In a city where no girl, ever, proposes to a boy, she had done the unimaginable. But her compromise did not seem to be acceptable to him.

Is that all he had to say? She asked herself, looking at the floor to hide her despair. She sorted out her thoughts for a few more moments, and said, "What if my mother refuses to pay for my stay?"

"Then you have to wait for me to come back," he answered.

"Wait? For two years?" She asked, shaking. "And how am I to explain this to the whole world who already knows about my affair? The word has been going around, and every one is assuming that we'd be getting married after graduation, including myself."

"Well, that is your problem. "

"This" was not what she had dreamed about for three years. Yet, it made no sense discussing it any longer.

"Okay, I'll try," she agreed, feeling as small as a needlepoint.

She had started it all wrong, and now, it remained seeking her mother's help, or sinking deeper into the swamp of indignity that she had just found herself in, up to the knees.

It was going to be a challenge. "He" did not fit in with her family's high social class, and that was a significant issue in the sixties in Iran. She was certain that her mother would reject the idea at once.

The best way to get Mom's approval would be to tell her the truth, she concluded. *I'll have to admit that I have been seeing him for some time.*

She had to take the blame for having fallen in love, and worse than that, he was an unsuitable man. But she chose to take it, for all she knew, it was right.

Intimidated, and unconvinced, she hung to the last reserves of her hope, and told her mother a slightly twisted version of the truth: that they loved each other, and "he" had asked her to marry him. And then the Germany problem. Her mother listened, stone-still. Then, in very few words she made it clear:

"There is no alternative. Money is not the real issue. We'll have to send you with him."

She froze. She had won the argument, but the victory did not taste sweet; it was bitter. Only then, the heavy walls of uncertainties surrounding her collapsed and she realized what damage she had done to her future. She was not even asked if that truly was what *she* wanted. And her cry for help was not so obvious. In the purity of her young world, it was beyond comprehension that she would be allowed to marry "the wrong man," just to avoid a scandal!

That was the way it worked then. Tradition and prestige were the main priorities.

It took her weeks to recover from the trauma of her discovery. Time ran out, and he left, leaving her behind to fight on her own.

The next shock came two months later. Amongst the love letters she received from him, there was a letter saying that *she* had to get in touch with his parents, and make them come to her mother to talk.

In keeping with tradition, the boy's parents would arrange a meeting to be held at the girl's parental home. In this gathering, they would ask for the girl's hand on their son's behalf. If the proposal is accepted, the next meeting is when the boy and girl would meet for the first time.

Nothing was going for her, the way she was accustomed to. It was up him to talk to his parents. That was the most embarrassing step he had asked her to take. She felt belittled and deceived. Yet, deep down in the hole she had found herself, that was the only way out.

So, she made the call or else there could be no wedding, and she would lose face with her mother, and the entire family.

"I don't want a wedding ceremony, and you don't need to pay for anything, but I have already told my mother that you'd be coming, please just come." She begged his mother.

And then came the disaster. His parents did not know of his intention to marry her. So they solidly refused.

When she put the phone down, she folded on the floor. She could not believe how cleverly he had made her bounce high and low, to keep up with the surge of his lies.

Crushed between his parents' disapproval, her mother's impatience for them to come, and his love letters from Germany asking why she was not coming, she did everything, that an ethical girl would normally not do. She put aside her pride and integrity and called them again and again, asking them to come.

Now that he was so far away, she had plenty of time to think. About all their fights, which he called lovers' quarrels. About his possessiveness that she took as a sign of love. The more she looked, the more clearly she could see his deceptions. She asked herself so many times, *was I wrong? Is he going to change after marriage?*

His parents' rejection upon rejection was rubbing salt into her injury. She felt unworthy and cheap; losing self-respect, she gradually lost the will to live.

The next few months she spent playing with the idea of suicide, exploring possible ways. The calming and satisfying feeling following such thoughts convinced her that it truly was the best for her.

Until one day, destiny saved her, through a message that came in a dream. A blessing, or more likely nature's cruelty, letting her know that not everything was up to her.

The day began with her Aunt Marin's telephone call. She invited her to spend the weekend with them. It was not out of the ordinary. They had done that before. Marin was the wife of her mother's brother. They had three children with whom they grew up. Their house was full of beautiful childhood memories for her. She accepted the invitation as she always did.

It was a quiet late summer evening; she enjoyed chatting with Aunt Marin and Uncle Mamud, through a peaceful dinner on the patio. Soon after she got up, worn out from the last few months of emotional strain, and excused herself:

"I am ready to go to bed," she said. "Thank you, Aunty, dinner was delicious. Good night all."

As soon as she finished complimenting, Aunt Marin rose, in a rush: "Wait for me, I have something to tell you," she whispered, joining her as she walked toward the guest-room. "In fact, your mother has asked me to talk to you. She wants you to understand that marrying this young man is wrong. He does not match our family. Listen," she said, "you are an intelligent young lady. You have been accepted at university, passing this difficult entrance exam. You know how many students wish to get in, and can't. Soon you can have your degree. He has nothing to offer you."

Marin paused here, caught her breath and continued; "Look at yourself in the mirror. Your beautiful hazel-brown eyes, your long wavy hair. It is a waste..."

"Is this *your* opinion about me?" She questioned impatiently.

"No. Everyone's. Look, there is this rich physician, a friend of your father, I don't know him. But he has asked your mother for your hand. What do you think?" They had reached the bedroom. Marin ended her long talk at this point and waited for her reaction.

Her response was unpredictable. "Oh, him! I know who Mom is talking about. He is fat and ugly, and much older than me." She revealed, and then paused to give Aunt Marin a chance to contradict. Nothing happened.

"This is about my future! Why mother did not talk to me herself?" She asked, even though she knew why.

None of the family members were accustomed to the way she was getting married. She did not see a reason why she should argue with her Aunt. *Why am I discussing this, while I wouldn't be living much longer any way*, she thought. This resolution cooled her down. So she turned to Marin and gazed through her eyes, as if talking to the air, "Do you want an answer tonight, Aunty?"

"Don't look at me like that, and enough with the nonsense." Marin interrupted.

"Right," she murmured as if she did not hear her aunt. "Tell mother I am not going to marry any of them. Good night, Aunty," she responded in a mystic tone of voice, just before she turned around and walked into the bedroom. "I won't live long enough to do that anyway," she continued in a voice so low that silent Aunt Marin could not hear it. Even the door did not make much noise so quietly that she closed it.

The dream came that night. She saw herself on her wedding night, in a glamorous wedding gown. The groom was the man they wanted her to marry. After the ceremony, they walked to the bedroom. There he went ahead, undressing her, leading her gently toward the bed. Then she saw herself naked on the bed, wondering what was going to happen next.

When it started to happen, and he rolled on top of her, she froze. Distressed and disgusted, she asked him to stop: "Oh no. Please let me go, I cannot do this!" But he went on. She kept asking, pleading him to leave her alone. It did not work. So she put up a hysterical struggle, screaming: "You can't do this to me! I don't want you. I won't let you waste my dignity. Leave me alone! Leave me alone!"

She was shrilling as hard as she could.

Like a butterfly guilty of its beauty, she was enslaved, fighting for freedom. But he seemed to be enjoying her resistance, and was fighting back. It went on until she almost lost. And just as he was about to take her, she jumped up, sweaty, frightened, and confused.

She sat up in her bed. Looked around, making sure it was only a dream. Then she burst into tears: "Oh God, help me, how could I marry someone I don't know?" She sighed desperately and went on, talking to the horror of the night: "I'm sorry Mother, I can't go through an arranged marriage. Please forgive me, but I'll have to go to Germany. I think he is the only person I could go to bed with, if ever."

That night she made up her mind. Germany became the only place of refuge for her now. A place where she could hide from it all. Even though it meant marrying a fake, she decided she would take it; whatever the future might hold.

So she decided to fight for something she thought was right for her, and someone she didn't believe in any longer. And she won. His parents finally agreed to come to her mother, under the condition that they do not pay for anything.

To win or to lose, -- two indefinable terms, when it comes to taking big risks in life. Only time can tell; and that, long after one can change anything.

Two months after surviving that demoralizing wedding ceremony, she was now flying to Germany to start her new life. Sex was utterly unknown to her. She was curious about it without any imagination. But she was determined to make the best of it, whatever might come. Her dream of having twenty-five children and grandchildren could become a reality now. The joy of making a beautiful home and creating a warm family life for them. The picture that filled her with happiness each time she imagined it.

She turned to her father. He was having his dinner. So were the other passengers. Her father had not said anything through the entire flight; he had tried to avoid eye contact with her. *"God knows what is going on in your mind, Dad, I love you dearly, and hope so very much that you will forgive me,"* she said to him, without words. *"I hope everything will work out,"* she thought to herself, looking at her untouched dinner on the tray in front of her.

Despite all the positive thoughts she tried to concentrate on, she still had a feeling that something was missing, and she could not put her finger on it.

Five years later, she found out what it was. It was only too late, at the wrong time, and the wrong man who guided her through the sweet taste of that missing piece of the puzzle.

CHAPTER 4
Just for My Daughter

It was midnight when they arrived at the enormous, busy Cologne Airport. A heavy fog hid the city; yellow streetlights could hardly be seen. Hugs and kisses in the cold and chaotic airport promised her a delightful start. They got into his little VW Beetle and headed to Solingen, the small town where he lived and studied.

They arrived after a long drive, and stopped by the hotel where her father would stay for a month before going back to Teheran. They all got out of the car. "Safe and sound," her father murmured, trying unsuccessfully to look at ease. He had made the journey only to see his young girl's safe arrival.

The hotel building was lost in the fog. All they could see were blurred inside lights here and there.

"Nobody seems to be here. Do I have to ring the bell?" her father asked, walking towards the closed door of the hotel, trying to hide his wet eyes and the bleak expression in his face.

"Yes. But they know you'll be late. Someone is waiting for you inside the building." She assured him. "We will wait here with you, and see you into your room," she added, helping him to end his misery, he did not want them to see.

On the second floor they entered a small room. Her father took a few steps in, but quickly turned around, grabbed their hands and put them in one another and said, "Have a good life, take good care of my daughter." They hugged, she said a quick goodbye, and then walked away with her husband, before her father could see "her" reduced to tears. And so, she started the married life, totally unaware of all what was coming.

She was hoping for a romantic evening and a quiet dinner, just the two of them. But to her surprise, when they arrived, three guests were already waiting for them in the flat. Two Iranian bachelors and a German girl who lived upstairs. "A welcome party for you," he said.

"Or my wedding night ceremony," she answered sarcastically.

It was her party. Yet, they all spoke German, so that the neighbor could understand. But she, the bride, the supposed guest-of-honor, did not understand a word. And her husband did not notice anything at all. They were having a great time; lots of loud talk and laughter, drinking and smoking, which went on forever. They had almost forgotten about her. As the night wore on, her presence dissolved into the thick smoky air. She was feeling lonely in the crowd, trying hard to put an iron lid on her anger, and a bitter smile on her face. Little by little, everything in the room started to turn around her head. Their voices began to sound like hundreds of flying bees, rushing out of four enormous red tunnels surrounded by pairs of giant purple lips. The music thundered like the clapping wings of a cloud of vultures, trying to poke her ears out, alive in the middle of a hot, barren desert.

Finally, "her party" was over, and they walked out of the house to see the guests leave. When everyone left, she could not hold back, "Was that supposed to be my party? Why did nobody talk to me or at least in Farsi? You and your friends know both languages."

Irritated, her husband began shouting, "They had come to meet you, and what do you do? You ignored them all night. You did that just to hurt me, you are jealous of my friends."

She was shaking, "Get your voice down," she demanded. "People can hear you."

"I don't care."

He truly did not care. Ironically, he was mad, accusing "her" of not having been more sociable and friendly to his guests. He was more concerned about his friends than her. In the heat of the argument he slapped her in the face, still standing on the pavement, while she was trying to make him understand that she did not expect her wedding night to start the way it did.

What happened that night was not their first quarrel, but it was the first time he struck her. It was the beginning of a bad dream.

She started crying, and ran inside. He followed her. As he saw her crying hysterically, he calmed down. Then he wrapped his hands around her, and asked her to forgive him. Softly, he wiped the tears off her troubled young cheeks, as he gently undressed her.

In the next few moments, she lost her virginity; the honor that she had reserved with pride and dignity all of her twenty years for the man of her dreams, the one she would love. Instead of tender endearments, it started with absurd and ruthless words: "I am going to fuck you now. I have been waiting for this for almost three years." And then it happened.

To her, it was nothing but a painful experience, and left her bleeding, hurt, and confused. *Is this what love is*? she asked herself, wondering. *Is this what sex is about*? That night she played her "part" as well as she could, like a good wife, as she had been taught to be.

Her husband showed his true face much sooner than she had expected. And it was worse than she had feared. He was a compulsive liar, bitterly jealous, and endlessly selfish. His friends were the most important elements in his life. He spent their entire small budget on traveling with them, or entertaining them. She was left home alone for days and sometimes weeks with no money, even for food. Those were the days she had to sneak into the property owner's cellar, where they stored onions and potatoes for winter, and took a few potatoes for food, to stay alive.

Each time she criticized his behavior an argument and then a fight followed, and it ended with her being beaten and left bleeding. On her long lonesome days, she spent her time reading his old love letters that she had kept hidden. They made her feel loved again and gave her renewed sense of hope. Evenings she spent watching TV, thinking and searching for a way to keep her husband home.

Months went by, and her uphill strive to create a friendly atmosphere to keep him at home went wrong every time. She just could not understand what she was doing wrong. Her unfinished dream castle was collapsing brick by brick. She was about to fail. Finally, she felt she could no longer bear all that agonizing pain in silence, *This frustration is going to destroy me, I need someone to talk to. But whom?*

She thought of confiding in her second sister, Shana. Shana was one year younger, and knew about her older sister's affair from the beginning. She had covered for her in all fairness. But when it came to dating, they somehow drew apart. It was wrong to talk to Shana about the sweet details of dating. On one hand, she was ashamed and would not want to encourage Shana to make the same mistake she did. While their mother constantly advised the girls to be careful and: "Not do what your eldest sister did." On the other hand, complaining to Shana now, she was sure would disappoint her young sister. She would not want that either.

But in the end she decided to break her silence, write to Shana, and tell her what was going on. She wished she did not have to do that, but what else?

She wrote four letters to her. Those letters caused a twist in their future beyond her expectations. And she did not find out how, until years later. It started shortly after she sent the fourth one.

First Letter

My dear Shana,

I don't want you to worry about me. I don't want answers to my letters, or give me advice. Just listen, and let me talk. Let me tell you about my experience one night shortly after I arrived, as Dad was still here. He only stayed for one month, remember? Anyway, sometimes I think I am punishing myself. Let me do it until I am satisfied that I have repaid what I think I owe to myself, to mother, and to our family.

It was late on a very cold night. After one of our usual fights, he kicked me out of the house! He said he didn't want me there anymore, and that I'd better go back to Teheran with Father. I suddenly found myself on the snowy, empty roads walking aimlessly in the dark. Here, in this small village of north Germany, almost everyone goes home before dark. They have to pull down the wooden blinds on the outside windows when it gets dark. House lights are not allowed to show from the outside. Maybe a habit that remained from the world wars. Anyhow, the roads are empty, silent, and grisly at night, especially in winter.

I did not know what to do. I walked around for a long while without knowing where I was. Finally I decided to go to Dad at his hotel. Of course I will return to Teheran with him, this is more than I can handle, I told myself. I knew that the hotel was nearby, and tried hard to remember how to get there. At some point, I asked a rushing passer-by for directions, in English. He said something in German, and pointed to the end of the road. It was not much help, so I continued walking and crying, my tears running uncontrollably down my face. A long while later I saw lights in the distance. I must be there, I thought, and began to run. But I was wrong; I was in the town center, nowhere near Dad's hotel!

Exhausted and frustrated, I walked up and down, turning right and left, determined to find the way to the hotel. I didn't want to go back to my husband anymore. After God knows how long, as I was passing a traffic light, I saw him in his car with the girl from upstairs. He shouted out of the window, "Where have you been? We have been looking for you all over the town." In that moment, I wished I could do anything to avoid getting into his car. But I did, and don't ask me why. What else could I do?

"Please drop me by Father's hotel," I asked him as I stepped inside. He did not answer, and five minutes later, we were back home in his place in absolute silence.

This time he did not even apologize. He mumbled hastily, "You see, you can't go anywhere without me, so cool down and put up with it." And threw himself on the bed.

Two weeks later Dad returned home without knowing any of this.

I didn't want him to. Well, this was the first adventure of my married life, not even a month after I had arrived. I don't have anything good to write about. I will if I find something.

I have to finish now. I beg you, please destroy my letters, don't write to me, and don't tell anyone what is going on here. I might sound stubborn, but that's the way I am.

Lots of love,
YourStupid Sister

As weeks and months were passing, her world was becoming smaller, and tighter around her soul. She was going through a deadly isolation and distress each day worse than the day before.

❖ ❖

Second Letter

My dear Sister,

He is not home most of the time, and I don't have anybody to talk to. I don't know the area, so I'm afraid to go out. I don't know the language, so I can't make friends, and besides he would not let me do any of these anyway.

Two weeks ago, we moved to a new place. It is a long story why, and I'll tell you all about it. It so happened that when I opened my eyes the day after arrival - after having lived in dreams and fantasies until then - I got really scared. The house we used to live in was a pre-war, two-story building. It looked like a big square cardboard box sitting upside-down, with only a few small windows so that we needed the lights on even during the day. Inside, everything was made of dark wood. The walls, the doors, the stairs. It was like living in a spacious coffin. The house belonged to a widow. She lived in the double bedroom with her only daughter; the other rooms were rented to students. We had a medium size room next to the owner's.

The furniture in our room included an ancient, wooden double bed that reminded me of John Wayne films, a small tabletop cooker on a little table, a huge three-door dark wood wardrobe, and a sink opposite the entrance door. You see what became of my dreams? This was where I started my new life; where I was pushed in roughly through the door by him, instead of carried in over the threshold. He, who said he loved me so much that he spent three years of his life to win me.

The owner and her daughter were both very kind to me, and they often asked me over. Although we didn't understand each other's language, we managed to communicate through sign language, and my dictionary. We grew to like each other very much. There was only a thin wall between our rooms, they would knock, and I'd go over. A few times, they asked me why I cried so often, for they could easily hear us. Each time I found something to say, like, I miss him during the day, or I miss my family, and more of the same lies. Until once, they apparently heard me crying all night. It must have been following one of our fights. This time I couldn't fool them. They didn't believe my stories anymore, and were not satisfied by my explanations, especially when they noticed his work on my body: scratches on my neck and face.

The next day they stopped him on his way out, and told him to stop beating me, or move out of the house. They were just feeling sorry for me, trying to help. But to my misfortune, it made things worse. From then on every time he beat me, he would put his hand over my mouth to stop me crying; so that no one can hear me.

One day he punched me in the nose. That time it felt like a man-to-man fight. It broke my heart; above the pain. My nose was bleeding, and he panicked. In an effort to keep me quiet, he made me sit on a chair and pulled my hair down at the back of my head to keep my nose up in order to stop the bleeding. But I could not breathe. The blood was running inside, blocking my airway until I was nearly choking. In a desperate attempt to get free I made a sudden move to the side, the chair gave in and I rescued myself only by losing a handful of hair. Then I ran out of the door shouting, "Help, please help me, I don't get enough air."

So that was it, and he had to urgently look for another place to live. Our new home is much smaller, and we got it on one condition: that I clean the owner's flat once a month, and the stairs from top to bottom once a week. I had no say in that; he did not even ask me beforehand. "Nothing else was available matching our budget," he explained later.

Well, that was the story of our move, and my making some friends. I don't think I can start a friendship with this new owner. She is an impossible, strange old woman with a coffee bitter face; you can't look at her longer than a second. She treats us like dirt, like most of them do, especially in my case as I don't speak their language. I must tell you the story of our first Saturday here so you can understand what kind of person she is.

According to the contract, she has to change the bed sheets every other week. That Saturday it was early in the morning, and we were still in bed. She charged in without knocking, and ordered us to get out of bed so she could change the sheets, as she had to take them to the laundry "now." Can you imagine that?

Sometimes I wish Mother had punished me herself, to protect me from destroying myself, instead of letting me go so easily. This is my feeling, I am sorry if I make you think I am being disgraced. But to tell you the truth I still have no regrets. I am going to try to make it work as long as I can.

Lots of love,
Your Sister

Two months later, she got pregnant without knowing it. When she asked him how it happened and reminded him that they had planned not to have children for the first two years. He answered carelessly with an ugly smile on his face: "I don't know. The condom broke."

"And you didn't let me know! Why?" He had no answer, so he

walked away.

She was four months into the pregnancy when she once, purely accidentally, experienced sexual satisfaction. For the first time in her life. It took her long to find out what was sex all about.

Third Letter

My dear Shana,

Let me give you the good news first: I am going to have a baby. I think I over-estimated my control over my life, and ignored the power of destiny. Now I believe that you either accept what comes your way, or fate is forced upon you. Just look at my life story! The baby is growing fast, and I am getting heavier every day. This human being inside me, moving like a fish and sometimes like a football player, reminds me that now I have somebody here with me and for me. It is such a reassuring feeling. It fills me with enormous joy and serenity. I don't know if it is a girl or boy, but it doesn't make any difference in the way I feel.

Now I have long hours of morning sickness with my head in the sink. Then I clean up, do the housework, cook dinner, make myself up, and fall asleep sitting at the dinner table, waiting for him to come home. The best times of the days are when I am reading his old love letters, which I still have kept in hiding! Or when I sit on the couch, with my hand on my big tummy and touch my baby, talking to it until it goes to sleep. I know when it sleeps because it stops moving. You know what? I nearly lost my baby a couple of times. The first time was when we were standing on top of the four steps leading to the garden, discussing something. He suddenly burst into one of his wild moods, and kicked my backside. I rolled down the stairs and lost consciousness. When I opened my eyes, I was in bed and he was gone. Little pieces of blue paper covered the floor; the love letters. He had found them, and torn them all to pieces, just to hurt me.

A few months later, I was going for a regular check-up and had to take the bus because he did not remember the date and left early in the morning. I was standing at the bus stop waiting in the cold and the frozen roads caused the bus to be late. I don't know what happened. I must have fainted, and fallen flat on the ground. When I came to, I was in bed in a strange house and a middle-aged man stood beside the bed looking at me carefully. "What happened?" I asked.

"You fainted," he answered. Then he gave me a pitiful look and said, "Don't you worry, my girl, I am a doctor, and you are all right. You were carried here by passing pedestrians. But tell me something, does your husband beat you?"

I gave him an astonished look. "How did you guess?" I asked, and pulled myself together, trying to be strong.

He smiled bitterly. "I told you, dear, I am a doctor. This is the reason you fainted. He must stop that," he added in a warm and fatherly tone of voice. That day I took a taxi home, and to this day I don't know who he was and where I had been.

It happened once again, when I was at home alone. I found myself lying on the bathroom floor: shaking. I was unconscious for a long while. The only thing I can remember is having felt sick and walking towards the sink. Since these incidents happened, I keep checking on the baby regularly to make sure it's alive. I promise you this; I will kill him if he does something to my baby. Only a few more months, and we will be there. Pray for me that he is at home when it comes, because we don't have a phone.

Lots of love and good-by for now,
Your Sister

Time passed as slowly as a worn out wandering turtle as she went through the emotional upheaval of her unplanned pregnancy. And she made it bravely through this most important time of every woman's life with no attention or support from him.

In the heart of an extremely cold winter night in January as the sky turned black and painted the snow that had masked the city a navy-blue color making it look like an enormous grave yard. When the blinking Christmas lights conveyed an untold contrast of hope and hopelessness, the pains began.

He took her to the hospital. In Germany in 1968 the hospitals did not permit the husbands to stay during the birth. "He can come back to see you tomorrow. You are going to be just fine," she was told.

Inside, she had to answer hundreds of medical questions and fill out endless forms. But she did not understand any of it. The pain was growing stronger and her strength lesser by the minute. She wished her mother or sisters were there to help her. Or somebody. Anybody.

After a while, a nurse examined her: "You need another two or three hours." So, she was taken to the "pain room."

The pain room was a small empty soundproofed room with a toilet at the end and nothing else. She couldn't believe her eyes. There was not even a chair. It was so designed that the patients sit on the toilet, and push, when the contractions began. So she did. And screamed and shouted, "Oh God please help me. I want my mother!" And yelled, begging for help. No response. So she cried and prayed and went through the contractions one after another.

It was all so different from what she had seen in her country. She remembered the times when she accompanied her gynecologist mother to deliver a baby. It happened either at home with the family members around, or in the hospital the same way. She was a little girl then. Even when her youngest brother was born, she could remember her mother's pain and screaming, but no loneliness. She was not so neglected like her now.

It took so long, well beyond her capacity to remember, until they took her to the delivery room. She was almost unconscious. Everything looked gray and blurred and the faces all alike. After placing her on the delivery chair, they all left except for one nurse who examined her again. And then she sat across the room and started knitting.

Her pain was growing unbearable, one attack after another as the pauses in between turned shorter and shorter. She was moaning, bending and stretching. And the nurse went on knitting, not offering a word of comfort, not talking, nothing. Suddenly, she felt the baby's head pressing hard to emerge. She shouted to the nurse: "It's there! Please help, the baby is there! I can feel it!" The nurse didn't even move her eyes toward her. At this hopeless moment, she heard the doctor's voice entering the room. "Okay, I think it is time." He came nearer, looking at her exhausted face and asked in Persian, "Are you Iranian?" She gave him a drained glance, a pale smile, and nodded using the last of her energy. Then she heard him say, "I'll be delivering your baby. Everything is going to be all right. Count to ten, and you will go to sleep."

A Persian! Where I least expected. The guardian angel, thank you God. A sigh of relief, and she closed her eyes. Gradually the noises started to fade away. And then, everyone and everything disappeared. Even the pain.

When she opened her eyes, the first thing she saw was the clock on the opposite wall. It was 7:30 a.m. She was still in the delivery room. No one was around. She checked her belly. Yes it was over. Her very first thought was of her mother. She needed her on her side so badly. She thought, *"Mom, I wish you were here and not so far away from me in soul and in body. I wish you didn't hate me because of my mistake."* No one was around, and she still didn't know if she had a girl or a boy. Soon she fell asleep again.

A noisy train passing outside woke her up. She found her self in another bed in the maternity ward. She couldn't remember how she had gotten there. A nurse put a tray of food beside her bed. She couldn't keep her eyes open; sometime later, another nurse took it away. It happened again and again, without her touching the food, and none of them seemed to be concerned.

The next day she was fully awake, waiting to see her baby. "Good morning," said a nurse, as she came in with something in her arms wrapped in a blanket, "Do you want to see your baby? It is a girl. What is her name?"

"Moosh," she answered. Then she saw her daughter for the first time. She was tiny, had brown eyes and a lot of black hair. As soon as she held her, the baby turned to her and opened her little mouth looking for food. "Oh God, how much I love you, little Moosh. I promise to be a very good mother for you," she said holding her daughter tight against her chest, patiently teaching her the first step how to feel the nipple and begin sucking. She was not feeling lonely anymore.

In that moment, she pledged to be a perfect mother, to give her baby the love, attention, and devotion that she herself had never received. She didn't know then that to keep her promise, she'd have to pay a unique price from the moment on when her daughter was born.

Her husband visited them in the hospital the second day. Sitting on the visitor's chair, he looked at her for a while emotionless. Eventually he expressed his thoughts: "It is a girl?" Then he turned his head toward the window, looking away from her and said: "Ah, I always wished for a boy. Whose child is she anyway? She doesn't look like me."

For the first time since they married she didn't feel hurt or even bothered by his chilling remark. He had become so transparent by then. She knew he enjoyed annoying her and watch her frustration. He took pleasure in her pain.

I won't give you the satisfaction ever again. I am going to fight you until my last breath, she thought, but to him she said: "I am not feeling well, thank you for asking, but if I was I would pull you off that chair and kick you out of the door."

Her reaction was too much for him. "Oh, are we feeling crafty now?" he questioned provocatively, raising his eyebrows up to his hair line. Then he stood up. "The nurse told me you would be released tomorrow. I'll be back to take you home." With those cold words, he walked to the door.

"Home? You call that place a home."

He had slammed the door closed.

❖❖ ❖❖

Fourth Letter

Dear Shana!

It's a girl . . . I named her Moosh. She was born on the seventh of January 1968. She has changed my life completely. I am a happy person again. She is my companion, my confidant, and my best friend, and I love her very much. I'm too occupied with her now to care about what he is doing, and probably won't have much time to write letters. I hope you'll understand.

There is something else I must tell you though before I finish, something bizarre. I had a letter from Mom about two months ago. She wrote: "We have been thinking. We could support both of you to stay in Germany for two more years, so that he can continue his course and get a degree." (His scholarship is only for two years and he would just be awarded a certificate at the end; not a degree.) "However," she wrote: "We would do this only if you are happy with him, and he is treating you right. If so, let us know. We'll make arrangements for sending the money."

You know, the more I thought about it the less reason I found to stay here for two or three more years, taking this torture, so that he can get his degree. For his future benefit? Or even mine? Neither he nor this marriage is worth sacrificing more than I already have. And I don't believe that a higher degree of education could enhance his character, or turn him (or anyone) into a decent human being.

I didn't want to stay here one day more than I had to. Because I was hoping that when we return, with all of you around, he wouldn't dare treat me like this. But how would I say that to Mother? Can you see my problem now? If I had refused their offer and said that I wanted to come back, Mother would have sensed that something is wrong with my marriage; that I am unhappy here. And I don't want her to know this.

Anyway, since her letter I'd been thinking and juggling the words without much success. How do I reply without letting Mom find out what is going on here? What reason do I use? Why else would I be refusing this excellent opportunity for both of us?

I honestly don't understand why I was never given the opportunity and the courage to tell Mom what I felt and what I wanted; to admit that I was drawn blindly in to this relationship. Do you believe me, that it was just an innocent relationship? Isn't it strange that I don't dare tell Mother the truth, even now? Is it I? Or maybe it's the fact that I know too well that she can't face the reality.

*Anyway, strangely enough, I got help from above. Before I came to a conclusion, I went into labor. Well, you are not going to believe this, but as soon as I saw my baby I had the answer. You see, everything is different now that I have a child. I don't think of myself anymore; for me, it is all about my baby. If I can endure two more years of suffering so he can get his degree, my daughter would have a reason to be proud of her father. For he has nothing to offer her the way he is behaving. I feel that it is up to me now to do something for my girl, so that she can look up to her father and be proud. I left the university and messed up my life by falling in love. But I can make it up to my Moosh now. And I feel I owe this to my baby. With her beside me, I'll have twice the power. I shall resist. Whatever may come. I know I can, as long as no other woman is involved in his life, and I give him credit for that at least. Believe me, he **CANNOT** lie to me in that department.*

I am going to write Mother that everything is fine with us, that I'm happy with him and accept their offer of financial help. Well, this means I will not see you all for some time longer. I am going to miss everything and everybody, especially you and Dad, but time will pass, I promise. Please don't forget to destroy my letters. And don't write to me. I don't want him to see your letters, and find out that I have told you what he is doing to me. I'd be in big trouble.

Love to all,
Your Sister

She mailed the two letters, one to her sister and the other, the delayed reply, to her mother. Finally, she had found a purpose and the peace of mind to go on.

Her pledge to her daughter began with that day. She chose to go for more years of torment, just for her daughter. All the love she had stored in her heart, the love her husband failed to see, feel, or enjoy, she decided to pour into her daughter's life. The satisfaction and happiness she now felt made her life worth living again.

One week later, after she had made up her mind, she told him about her parents' offer. For him, it was a dream come true. He was ecstatic as she thought he would be, but hardly appreciative. She did not care at all.

That day she had no idea that soon she would lose her newly found sense of fulfillment. Somewhere far away, a trusted person would cause a twist in her life through a single incident. Distant events would deceive her and the web of destiny would change her brave and carefully made plans.

It started with a telegram that she received from home one month later. It read: "Call home immediately, it's important." She was surprised and somewhat suspicious. She thought, *Why do I have a feeling that it can't be good news? I hope Dad is all right. I'd better find out quickly.*

She got ready in a hurry, put the baby in the stroller and walked to the post office to make the call. Luckily, it was a quiet time of day so she didn't have to wait long.

Her mother answered the phone. "Hi Mom, it is me. Is something wrong?"

"Nothing is wrong. I just wanted to tell you that I am sending you a ticket. I want you back home as quickly as possible."

"But why, Mom? Did you not say we could stay two more years; did you not receive my letter? I said it is all right with me, I--"

Her mother interrupted, "Yes we received your letter, but there has been a change of plan. There are no financial problems; nobody is ill, nothing to worry about. Talk to your Dad, your sisters and brother now, and make sure."

"Then why do you want me to return so urgently? Can I at least wait and come back at the same time with him? He finishes his current course in a few months." She paused for an explanation, but her mother wasn't there anymore. Instead, her sister said, "Hi sweetie. . ."

She talked with the whole family, one by one, but none of them knew why her mother had changed her mind. And so, the conversation ended. She hung up more puzzled than before, and carried the stroller and her crushed self out of the post office, ignored by the girls behind the counter.

On that sunny cold February day she pushed the stroller forward and walked away from the thin lines connecting her to home and to her mother whom she needed so much, but was far away.

Outside: every house, every car, and every person looked like an enormous question mark to her. She was in no hurry to go home and break the bad news to her husband. Gloomy, she walked past the house and up the narrow walkway, which led to the small park nearby.

The park was crowded when she arrived. Younger couples were walking up and down the alleys. The older ones were sitting on the wooden benches chatting. Children were playing noisily on the brownish yellow meadow. The path continued into endless woodland behind the house. She used to watch that green spot from her bedroom window, where she sat and gazed at the outside world for hours through her long, lonesome days.

Hurt and enraged, she was looking for a quiet place to vent her anger. She could find no excuse for them to make such a decision for her without consulting to her. She walked further, well into the heart of the forest until a flourishing plane tree attracted her. She parked the stroller under the tree, took the baby out carefully, placed her cozily in her arms, and settled herself under the branches.

"Why, Mom? It is not about me. How am I ever going to make him understand? He won't allow me to toy with him like this. I'll have to take the consequences. And what about my daughter?" She went on, talking loudly to the weeds and the enormous gray stems of the aged trees in her eyesight:

"Mother, this time, it is going to be a disaster. He is going to go wild and tear me apart." Her voice grew louder and louder as she freely argued, complained, and shouted out all the words she'd kept inside. For no one could hear her, not even the green leaves of the tree above her head. They were too busy making rustling noises in the wind.

At last, she calmed down and gave up. There was nothing she could do to change things now.

A swift chilly breeze touched her face and brought her back to where she was. She realized she had been sitting there for hours, not noticing anything around her. It had become ominously quiet. Time to go back. She looked around, it was twilight and she couldn't see far. The dark-blue clouds in the sky were pregnant with a heavy downpour. The baby was asleep in her arms. She put her in the stroller to leave before complete darkness, and aimed to walk out of the lonely forest.

When she heard the sound of thunder in the distance, she walked faster trying carefully to retrace her steps. When the rain caught up with them, she pulled the stroller's shade open to protect her baby from rain, and ran. But soon she was stopped by a fork in the road. "Which way did I come from?" She asked herself desperately. In her state of panic, she couldn't remember anything. She looked around for someone who could give her directions. But as far as her eyes could see, she was the only person there. She had to decide one way or the other, so she did.

But just before she moved, a mass of dense fog plunged down and blocked her vision, threatening like a hungry gray bear. It suddenly got much darker, and the fork in front of her disappeared in the artificial night. At that point, she just ran, scared, not knowing where she was going or which path she had taken.

Half an hour later, she noticed a moving shadow in the distance. It looked like a man with a gun on his shoulder. She thought, *this person can either show us the way, or rape and kill us. But lost here, we'll freeze to death. So I'll take the risk and ask him to show me the way out.*

"Excuse me, sir, can you hear me? I think I am lost, could you show me the way to the park please?" She shouted with all the strength she had left. The man stopped, took his gun off his shoulder, and turned around. He took a few steps towards her. She couldn't see his face.

"In God's name, my dear girl, what are you doing in this part of the forest this time of night? Don't you know that wild animals live in this area? They could have attacked and killed you by now." His voice sounded like a middle-aged man.

"No, I didn't," she answered in a low and exhausted voice.

"Come with me, this way. I am the forester, and I'm heading out too. You were going the wrong way."

She had no alternative. So she followed the stranger, walking a few steps behind him expecting the worst hoping for the best, and praying as hard as she could.

Through the long, wearisome walk that seemed like a life-long to her, lady luck began to join her step by step. The rain that had been pouring down like a waterfall from the sky, stopped. The dense fog uncoiled to mist. And little by little the moon reached out to help; penetrating cylinders of dim light through the holes in the clouds and the green roof of the trees into the mist. Although she was wet all over, she could see more of the surroundings now and the tiny drops of water that were dancing in the air around her. She was walking through a hazy green tunnel, trying not to lose sight of the forester.

The first thing she saw clearly, after a never-ending walk, was hundreds of colorful shiny stars not too high above the ground. She recognized the lights in the park. There she knew that once again an angel had helped her survive.

"There, that's the main road. Do you know how to get home from there?" The forester asked, pointing to the chain of lights not far away.

"Yes sir, I do. You don't know how much I appreciate your help," she answered. She still couldn't see his face.

"Don't mention it. Take care of the baby, it's cold," the forester said, raising his hand to say good-by. He then turned around and vanished in the mist.

Her husband wasn't home when they arrived. Weeks passed and she didn't dare tell him about her mother's change of heart, until she ran out of time. When she eventually told him, he went crazy as she had expected.

Paralyzed, she sat in the corner crying quietly while he turned the room upside down. The cookware, their clothing, the linens, he threw them all on the floor. He was kicking, punching, and shouting: "It's all your fault! You must have told your mother some bad things about me. That's why she changed her mind."

The baby started screaming. He paid no attention. She tried to explain. He wouldn't listen. So she just sat there rocking the cradle to calm the baby waiting for him to finish and storm out of the house.

One month later, her ticket arrived. She had to go back home, with her baby, as she was told.

On the departure day, he took her and their daughter to the train station to go to the airport. He was sulky all the way and wouldn't talk to her. She was restless and sad.

At the station, he told her that she must leave the stroller behind. "We couldn't afford to pay transport fees for this thing!" He sneered as he saw her disappointed face.

"But if you had told me, I would have asked my father for some extra money for it." He only shrugged. "Well it's too late to talk about it now."

It was too hard for her, dumping that significant part of her baby's short life! It felt like cheating a dear friend. A friend who had accompanied her all over the town, since the baby was born.

So she looked around until she spotted a safe place out of sight, near a wall. She pushed the stroller there cautiously and took the baby out. Then she stood there, staring at the stroller. She went through all the good moments they had together. Just the three of them, the baby, the stroller, and her. She remembered the night when they arrived home after that dangerous walk through the forest. How determined she was, pulling this weighty comrade up the narrow stairway to take it inside the flat so she could dry and clean it properly.

"You'd better hurry up or you'll miss the train," she heard him shouting. She pushed herself away from that trustworthy corner and got onto the train after bidding him a short good by. He was not going to the airport with them.

The regular motion of the crawling train took her mind off the harsh reality. The repeating noise of the engines sounded like a lullaby to her ears. She let her head fall on the back of the seat, closed her eyes, and disappeared from the busy world around her. She had surrendered, accepted to go along with the unpredictable way her life was being shaped by others' wishes and strange circumstances.

The airport looked the same as eighteen months before, when she first arrived. Only more crowded and chaotic. She could see herself arriving with her father, feeling lonely, but full of hope. Now she was there again, going back home heart-broken with just a little hope left in a small corner of her heart. But she was not lonely. Her daughter was with her.

"Ladies and gentlemen, welcome to Iran Air flight number.."

A few blissful tears warmed her cheeks as she heard the voice of the flight attendant. That familiar voice speaking in German with a Persian accent was a gentle music to her awaking sentimental forgotten feelings in her heart. The sense of belonging and the warmth of unity. She could even smell the familiar aroma of fresh backed "Sangak," the large, thin-crust bread that they used to have with every meal. The scent of wet, hot asphalt under the first rain-storm of Fall rising with the damp. The vintage aroma of her mother's Jasmines, all spring and summer long every early morning. And her honey-suckles, every evening. She began to feel lighter and lighter. She was flying high above the clouds, even before the plane took off.

PART III
BACK HOME

CHAPTER 5
The Most Regrettable Choice

As she saw the enormous landmark of Tehran's Mehrabad Airport from the sky and the millions of colorful lights of the city, she felt butterflies in her stomach. She knew they would be landing in Teheran any minute now. When she finally walked out of customs, she was drained. But as she saw her family in the distance waiting for her, she felt lively again. Her sisters were almost screaming, applauding and cheering:

"Look, there she is. With her baby," one said. "She's cut her hair short." They were showing her to each other. "She looks so beautiful."

"She doesn't look like a mom." That was her surprised brother.

None of them had changed much except her brother. His face had a shadow of thin, black hair, but not too much to need shaving. When she walked out towards them she saw her father and mother. Her father was looking her way, but he didn't react. She walked passed him, turned behind him and said, "Good to see you Dad."

Startled, he spun around, "Oh dear, I didn't recognize you. You have changed!" He said, in utter disbelief.

Her excited sisters got hold of her Moosh. So, she hung herself on her father's neck. "I'm so glad you are all right. So ... glad ... so glad, Dad," she went on and on, not willing to let him go.

"Where is the baby," the exited grandfather asked.

"I don't know, I think they took her with them, maybe in Shana's car."

"Let's go I want to see my grand-daughter." She let go of him and they walked out of the arrivals lounge. It amazed all of them that their father had not recognized her, but not her; with the two black circles under her eyes, she *did* look horribly different.

"I'll go in your car," she said to her father. She didn't see her baby again until they arrived home.

After the initial excitement and a week of sleep and rest, she began her search asking her sisters why she had been ordered to return home. No one knew anything. Much later she did find out, but too late.

She was now back in the same house where she had spent her teenage years. The same place where she experienced the racing heart and the fever of what she once called love. The same part of the world where her disappointment was conceived, even before her marriage. And the same bedroom where she had made up her mind to sacrifice herself for the family values.

Four months later her husband arrived. But he wouldn't stay for long. He had to leave home within two weeks to begin his military service, a compulsory two-year duty in Iran. During this time, men were usually sent to remote villages far from where they lived, receiving only a place to stay and pocket money.

She didn't mind his departure, hoping that the discipline in the military would help him cherish the value of family life that he didn't appreciate. But his absence meant two years of hard work for her. She had to provide for all three of them during the entire time of her husband's service. But challenge didn't intimidate her.

He left and the young mother and her baby stayed behind. She was on her own again, looking forward to quiet times ahead. He visited them twice a month on weekends.

During his absence, her main support was her father. He helped her morally and financially to ease the burden of her first few months, without making her feel embarrassed.

Her father was a humble, always calm and quiet man. His eyes bespoke his honesty, and she could see through his impassive face into his love and warmth. He would never express himself in words, as if he didn't exist for himself at all. When he was pleased, she could tell by his unique and reassuring smile that slightly lifted only one side of his lips. She loved him dearly and respected him eternally. But still, she never realized how much he meant to her until he left them for good.

Unlike him, her mother was remote, caught up in the sweet taste of professional success. She was the first female gynecologist in Iran of the forties. An era, where an educated woman was rare, let alone a working woman. And she tried hard to encourage her children to do the same. She was fifty-two then, full of extremes. An intellectual, matter-of-fact lady. The words "love," "feelings," or "emotions" were not in her lexicon. Although she was in love with worldly glamour and with herself, she constantly helped those in need. But she would mention it too often. She truly believed in God, "the Creator of the world," and was a religiously correct person.

Her mother and she lived in the same house, but each in her own world. Two totally different worlds. Little Moosh received a second-hand baby bed next to Mom's, after Shana moved to another bedroom. Nothing else changed in the house.

Soon after her husband left, she found a good job at the Ministry of Science and higher Education, while their live-in maid took care of her Moosh. She took the same public bus to work that she used to take to school when she was a teenager. The same bus on which she met her husband for the first time. It was depressing how things had developed since that time. And how she always went back, not in time, but to the starting line of her life's race. It happened again and again. She could not avoid the complex screenplay of her life.

In the summer of 1969, almost a year later, things changed very unexpectedly. That summer the family decided to take a vacation by the Caspian Sea for three weeks. At the resort where they used to spend their holidays every summer, just like the old days. Only this time they were accompanied by the two new members: little Moosh and the son-in-law. He was to join them in a week's time for ten days. She had worked hard for over a year now and was looking forward to spending time with her family on the beach. But, at the last moment her mother made known that she would not be going with them without an explanation.

Mom doesn't like to be around my husband and me, she had to assume. *Or is there something going on between her and Dad?* But she had learned not to ask questions.

They left without her mother. Her father drove the car. He was silent most of the way. Still, he was the only person in the world that she could enjoy his company in total silence. Neither of them were much of a talker. But that day the profile of his august face that she could see from the opposite side of the back seat where she was sitting, was talking to her. She could see through the little lines around his eyes and his unique one-sided smile the signs of contentment in his face. The face of a man with a heart as big as the whole world. His skinny, sagging double chin and the wrinkled skin of his bony hands, holding the steering-wheel revealed his fifty-two years of age and thirty years of working tirelessly for his children. He seemed excited about spending time with his granddaughter, but looked a little sad. *It is because Mom is not with us,* she told herself, *but he is enjoying the scenery.*

It was a wonderful drive. The winding road led way up, to the top of the mountains, then through a long tunnel to the other side. From there it went downhill curving around the mountains to sea level. They were The Elburz chain that lay from the Northwest to Northeast of the country, with their world-famous tip called the Damavand Peak. They divided the landscape into two contrasting climates. Dry and hot in the South, and evergreen, moist, and warm in the North.

Passing through the long and dark, drizzly tunnel, straight through the stony mountains was an exciting experience for them each time. To enter the tunnel hot and sweaty, and then come out into the moist air was an adventure they always looked forward to. The North was green. Everywhere and everything: The earth, the land, the hills and even the air looked green, in a way.

And then, that familiar scent filled the air; the scent of the sea and the blossoms of the orange trees standing in perfect rows along the sides of every street and each lane.

They had three wholesome weeks in that beautiful seaside resort. Her baby was eighteen months old now. Little Moosh was her joy and happiness and gave her all the reasons to go on. She lay on the sandy beach under the hot sun watching her daughter digging in the sand.

Her husband had been much nicer and understanding to her since he'd been away, and she assumed that the hardship of duty time had truly worked, and their bad days were over. So she thoroughly enjoyed the time with her husband and the family that she had missed for two years.

On their return, her mother was not home. Only a note that said, "I am going to The Damavand Summer Resort with a friend of mine and her family. You can join us if you like. This is the address . . . ." Her mother's cat and mouse play was unnecessary, but not unusual. So she decided not to join them. *It's better for Father to go alone so they can talk in peace and solve their problems, if that's the case,* she thought. So her father left and she stayed behind. But the events that happened following his short trip made her regret her decision for the rest of her life.

Two weeks later, on the weekend that her parents were to return home, she carefully gathered her father's shirts to wash and iron them ready for him to go back to work the next day. He was the physician to the 'Royal Guard' and paid careful attention to his appearance. So she got busy putting his shirts in the washer. When the cycle was finished, she looked inside and received an unpleasant surprise, the first sign of impending disaster. All her father's white shirts had taken a pinkish color. As she was taking the load out, she discovered one of her baby's little red shirts. It had remained in the machine from an old load and was not color fast.

It was devastating. *What am I going to do now? He is going to be furious at me. He's got nothing left to wear tomorrow. And the shops are closed today and I can't even buy one for him.* She was completely frustrated. She put so much weight on her father's opinion of her. *This is the worst that could happen to me, a perfect daughter. How am I going to explain this?*

By late afternoon she heard the car entering the garden. It was time. But strangely, her mother was alone. She was somehow relieved thinking: *What a delightful coincidence. Father has stayed longer, now I can buy him some new shirts.*

"Hi everybody. I'm back." She heard her mother shouting as she walked into the building. "Everybody gather in my bedroom, I have an announcement to make."

This is so like Mother, always making a big deal of everything, she thought. But the word "announcement" worried her. "*I hope it is nothing serious.*" She was thinking as she rushed down the stairs.

But what her mother had to say was nothing any of them could have expected. When they were all gathered, and just before her mother could begin one of her long speeches, she quickly told her what had happened with Father's shirts in anticipation of her support.

Disinterested, her mother began her talk, "I want all of you to listen to me very carefully. Pull yourselves together. Take this calmly. No screaming. No shouting. Anyone who feels like crying should go to her bedroom and cry quietly. I don't want to hear it." She paused, caught her breath, looking into their impatient silent faces, one after another. Then she suddenly got to the point: "Your father died yesterday, following a stroke in Damavand."

The rest of her mother's words were unclear to her. For she could only hear her own screaming from within, *he won't need his shirts any more.* And again. *He won't need his shirts any more,* again and again. She stood there, grief-stricken unable to move, until she could cry with dried tears.

He died far away from home, after God only knows how bad a fight with Mother, and none of his beloved children around him. She never, ever got rid of those thoughts. And every time they came to her, a painful sensation filled every cell of her body burning like a glowing piece of iron.

Her father's sudden, premature death, was her first experience with the departure of a loved one. On that day she lost her idol. The only person who was always there for her. Now, she had no one to lean on any more, not now, not ever again. He had gone.

During the next six months, she lived in a trance. She was totally lost, detached from everyone and everything around her. Her heart burned each time she remembered that she wouldn't see him again, beating wildly, like a little red fish thrown out of water. Soon after that, the temporary peace in her life shifted forever.

CHAPTER 6
The Betrayal

Her mother, now the head of the family, decided to give up her job and stay home to take care of the **children**! Three girls ages twenty-three, with a baby--the first-- next one twenty-two and the third girl twenty-one, and the boy of sixteen. *A good decision,* she found, *but much too late for the girls.*

Five months passed. In January 1970, her daughter Moosh turned two years old. Her youngest sister was now at the university and her brother still at school. Shana had graduated from university and was thinking of marrying her boyfriend, whom their mother didn't approve of. But when they threatened to do it any way, she gave in. "This" caused even more damage to the relationship between their mother and her eldest daughter. In her eyes, Shana was following her older sisters' footsteps, and that was unforgivable.

When the time came, everyone in the house was busy preparing for the wedding ceremony. Shana always dreamed of a glamorous wedding. She was that way, hungry for constant attention, seeking everything that dazzled the eyes. And her husband gladly paid for it. She was truly happy for Shana whose dream of having the kind of ceremony she wanted was coming true.

Finally, on the day her sister was moving out, she hopelessly asked her for the last time what their mother's motivation had been in calling her back from Germany. Shana was the only person who had the letters, and the only one who knew about her private life in Germany.

She found her in a quiet moment in the hallway and asked, "Shana, before you leave, please tell me what happened. I can't rest until I know."

Shana gave her a pitiful look. "But you must promise not to react aggressively."

"I promise."

"Look, I know you always told me in your letters that I should destroy them. Well, I didn't. God knows why. But I had them hidden under the couch so nobody could find them."

She felt a knot in her stomach. "Okay. I know. I can guess what happened. Mom sneaked in your room, as usual, and found them."

"Yes." Shana looked guilty. "But honestly I didn't realize that they were missing at the time. Your letters stopped, so I never went back to hide a new one. Until now, as I was clearing my bedroom, they weren't there. I promise you, I didn't show them to Mom. And I never told her anything, as you wished. Believe me."

"I believe you."

Shaking inside, she left Shana, and ran up the stairs to her room. There she sat by her baby's bed, and let her tears run. She had so much to argue with her mother, but words were frozen in her mind. *Mom, I'd have understood if you had told me that you wanted me back because he was abusing me. But I wished to stay. Just like "you" were trying to rescue me! I wished to do the same for my baby's future. I could have let you know, if only you'd asked me; that it was easy for me to take all that horror, knowing I was doing it for my daughter's benefit. I love my girl as much as you love me.*

As strongly as she felt, she knew she would never confront her mother. Nothing could make a difference now. Her chance was lost long ago.

When her sister moved to her new home, the house felt empty. But her husband would soon finish his service and return. In the hope of having him back and employed, she too began dreaming of moving to her own home. She was looking forward to a fresh start in her marriage.

If I could bring him a boy he so much wants, things might change for better, she naively thought. Anything to make him happy so he would stay. Anything to secure a proper family life for her daughter. A final effort to make her marriage work. So, in April 1970 when he came back permanently, she was two months pregnant.

All three of them now lived in her old bedroom on the second floor of her mother's house. He soon found a good job, and she naturally continued working to help build the family's resources. After a few quiet months her husband found out that her mother had taken over managing the family's considerable income from rental properties. He started chastising, "Why work? Just ask your mother for your share of the money. We could rent a flat and move out! Then, you can stay home and take care of the children."

This was a disclosure of yet another side of his ugly attitude that he'd kept from her. She had no answer for him. There were many details she couldn't tell him about; Her mother's dislike for him because he was not a "somebody" with a title, and for her, as she had not married one who was. And he would not accept her simple explanation: that she preferred to die rather than asking her mother for money. And her efforts to make him understand fell short time after time.

Slowly, their talks on the subject changed to endless discussions and then turned into fights. Until one day he hit her brutally, and left home again. She kept it all to herself and covered his absence with white lies that she told everyone, including her sisters. She was too ashamed talking about it.

Day after day she would put a smile and layers of makeup on her face and go to work. On the job everyone knew her as "the girl who never complains and always smiles." Her evenings were spent with her daughter. And at night when she was finally alone, she prayed: *May he change for the better, may her baby be a boy to give him a reason to change.* Praying was her solace. At such time that technology was not so advanced in Iran to know the baby's gender beforehand, her sole recourse was her prayers.

She strongly believed that there was someone up there who would help her, somehow. She was reminded often by the signs she received and angels who rescued her.

One night she received another spiritual message in a dream. That night she was so worn out, physically and mentally, that she fell asleep in the middle of her prayers. Then she dreamed of her father. The three of them were sitting by the fireplace together. Her father had the fire poker in his hand, holding it in the flames. When it turned red and began glowing, he took it out turned to her husband and shouted, "You! stop hurting my daughter or I'll kill you."

She could remember every detail of the dream the next morning. She had never seen her father so furious while he was alive. *Dad, you are still there for me. You are watching over me. I knew you wouldn't leave me on my own. Thank you, Dad.* The dream assured her somehow, that he was going to help her, that things would change sooner or later.

She was right. He was there for her, this time and every time she needed him.

In November when her second baby was due, her husband was still away. She was at work when the contractions began. She called Shana at work, who was nine months pregnant herself. "I think it's time. Will you drive me to the hospital?"

"Sure I will. But how can you tell?"

"I am bleeding, I've been through this before. I know it."

"Okay then, I'll be there in half-an-hour."

Shana drove her to the hospital. All the way she was still praying silently, *Dear God, please don't disappoint me. Let it be a boy."*

The birth was very different from the first one besides the fact that her husband wasn't there. She went through natural childbirth, but now she could talk to the nurses and tell them how bad the pains were. Her mother delivered the baby in the same hospital that she worked. So she was getting more attention and moral support from everyone.

"Mom, how long is this going to take?"

"Whenever the pains become so strong that you start biting your pillow and tearing it apart with your teeth," she joked. So, she pushed, squawked and groaned while the baby was pressing, and complained at every pause for four hours until finally she heard her baby's cry. The sound of that cry ended all her pain. She instantly raised her head to see what it was. As they were holding the baby upside down, she saw her little boy for a split second just before she felt the warmth of his little body on her belly while the nurse cut the cord.

And so Roy was born, with almost blond hair and gray eyes, without his father's presence, but a lot of love and support from her family.

Surprisingly, a few hours later Shana was delivered to the same hospital. And she too gave birth to a baby boy the day after Shana's first. The two sisters spent three days in the hospital in the same room. There were jokes, talks and laughter there. Three days of crowded party went on in that room as their youngest sister, and Shana's husband joined them and stayed with them most of the time.

The two boys would grow to become close friends, apart of being cousins.

The day they were being released from the hospital, after their mother had paid her hospital bills which were due same day, her husband appeared. Shana had told him where she had been. The miracle of having a son did seem to work. He stayed.

With Roy's arrival they were given a second bedroom. The four of them were now living in two bedrooms in her parents' house, along with her youngest sister and her brother.

Life upstairs was like living in a prison cell for her. The excitement of the births didn't last long for her mother. She returned to her old self again, pretending that her oldest daughter didn't exist. She turned a deaf ear to what she heard from the second floor. Nor did she ever offer help to her desperate daughter who cried out in the night, just above her bedroom.

The children were growing. But the peace she had so hoped for didn't last long. She requested, then asked, and finally begged her husband to get a place of their own.

"Only if you stop working," was his answer each time.

"But do you promise me to provide for us? You have a good income. If you don't spend it entertaining your friends, it'll be more than enough."

"You have enough money of your own, get it from your mother! Why should I give you any money?" And he'd accuse her: "You only work as an excuse to spend your time with the boys in the office. You don't **want** to quit."

Eventually, she reached the end of her tether and decided to take the risk. *If this doesn't work, and I am sure it won't, there will be nothing left that I haven't done to save my marriage,* she thought. So, she told her mother of her dilemma and asked her for help, something she felt ashamed of for the rest of her life.

Her mother listened unmoved, staring at her in disbelief with a faint cynical smile in her face. She was so certain that her daughter was lying that it didn't seem as if she was truly listening.

"Now you want to give up work and become a homemaker? You have sunk so low? For him?"

"I don't want to, I have to," she tried to make herself understood. But in her mother's eyes a woman, who did not work was not worth anything. She believed so strongly in her point of view that her daughter's reasoning was just nonsense to her.

She could *tell* from her mother's face expression, and hated herself having asked her. It had been an open secret between them. She knew too well that her mother had no respect for her or her marriage.

How stupid of me to hope that she'd understand, she was thinking as her mother continued, enraged, "I won't give you anything. If you are thinking of receiving your inheritance and giving it to that husband of yours to waste it all, you'd have to take me to court."

She knew all a long that it was wrong asking her, all the same, she wasn't expecting such a fierce reaction and those words. That evening she told her husband of her mother's response. He didn't believe her either.

"You are lying. You never asked. I can't imagine why your

mother wouldn't want to help you."

She was pushed in the corner, "Neither do I, but what else can I do?"

"Go to hell," he said. And he was gone, this time for three months.

Like a character in a cheap movie he kept repeating his sordid acts. And she merely watched as he continued leaving and coming back. Each time he'd return, he'd just walk in and say, "I forgive you," and stay. Then, within a couple of months after they'd gone through the same conversations and fights, he would beat her up and leave again. Their fights were becoming more frequent during his periods at home, and he was growing increasingly violent. He had turned her life into bloody warfare.

In one incident -- one that still hurts remembering to this day -- he threw her on the floor trying to strangle her. She attempted to push him away, but his heavy weight made it impossible. She was nearly suffocating. After a long struggle, she managed to slip to the side and narrowly escaped. She ran out of the room, and held the door closed on him with all her strength. *Where should I go now?* she asked herself desperately, *downstairs to Mother?*

In a split second, she could see her mother's reaction, and hear her voice in her mind: *Shame on you and your violent life. What have I done to deserve this?*

No, she thought, *not downstairs.* So she ran through the adjacent room. From there, she went out onto the balcony, which spanned both bedrooms and overlooked the side-yard and the narrow street below.

When he saw her through the large closed window, frustrated by his failure, he looked for something to throw. All he could find was a thermos on the table. He grabbed the thermos, raising it above his head, he threw the thermos toward her through the glass window.

The thermos hit her along with a rain of broken glass that poured over her. The shards cut her all over, some pieces imbedded in her bleeding flesh.

Her mother, having heard the noise of breaking glass, reacted. "What is going on up there?" She shouted. As soon as her husband heard her voice, he ran out of the house, leaving his injured wife to clean herself up. After she heard the door slam, she broke into tears. Then, she washed her face and her wounds and walked shamefully down the stairs to her mother's room.

"What was that? Who broke the window?" Her mother demanded.

In a barely audible voice, she told her what had happened.

"This is too much. I've had enough of this. We're going to the police right now." She was threatening.

At the police station, the officer advised filing a complaint, if they wanted him arrested. Her mother remained silent. And let her do the talking.

"No, I can't send the father of my children to jail," she argued.

"Then there is nothing we can do," the officer explained.

One month later he was back. By then he knew very well that she wouldn't press charges because of the children. So he kept returning. He wanted her, but only on his own terms.

Then, one day, an unfortunate event turned into a blessing; but it set fire to her heart before it did.

It all started at the end of a working day, when he was late picking her up from her office. She was waiting for him restlessly, thinking loudly, *"He should have been here by now."* She looked at her watch. *"I am sure I told him the right time that I would finish work today. Tthe children are waiting."*

One of the office girls noticed her concern. "Do you want a ride home?"

"No. Thank you," she answered. "You see, he'll go mad if he comes and I'm not here." And silently she thought *I'd be beaten to death tonight.*

"Why don't you call him at work, see if he's left." The office girl sympathized.

She grabbed the phone angrily. "I think I'll do just that."

As she was dialing, she was unaware that fate was pushing her toward another big change in her life.

The phone rang twice, then she heard his voice in the background, talking.

"Halloo, halloo, it's me," she shouted.

But he went on, as if he could not hear her. Suddenly there was a woman's voice. "She" paused, and listened. It was a mix-up in the line! Her husband and the woman were talking to each other and could not hear her. She recognized the female voice. It was her husband's cousin. So, she remained silent and listened to the entire conversation between her husband and his cousin.

At the end his cousin asked, "When am I going to see you again?"

"Same place same time tomorrow."

"All right, I'll see you then."

When they hung up, she too let go of the receiver, shattered.

After all she had endured to keep her marriage intact, this was the ultimate insult. She felt like her heart was being squeezed, pushing boiling blood through her veins to her face, burning her ears. For long moments she remained sitting still, paralyzed, with her eyes fixed on the phone. She could not move, feeling crushed and helpless as if buried alive following an earthquake.

Then, suddenly she jumped up and opened a drawer in search of her Aspirin tablets. She used to keep them there for her unbearable headaches. She had fifty of them. She grabbed the container and dragged herself towards the lady's room.

The office girl, who was watching her, became suspicious. She asked herself, *She said halloo twice and then just listened? It doesn't make sense. And then, that horrid look on her face! Where did she go now? Something isn't right.* She ran after her, and followed her into the rest room. There, she found her, standing by the sink, and trying nervously to swallow the Aspirins with the pipe water gathered in her clenched hands.

It was a miracle. The phone connection, this oldest invention of the new technology, had to "malfunction" in order to give her the message. The stars, the moon, the whole cosmos lined up perfectly to help her find out where she was standing.

It was a disturbing experience that nearly took her life. But a stranger saved her, so she'd pay the price, a prolonged excruciating pain, and then gain the freedom she deserved.

Later that night she confronted him. He denied everything. "Do you want me to believe all that rubbish? You heard me on the phone dating my cousin while you were dialing my office? Impossible! I am not that stupid to fall for this nonsense."

She couldn't blame him. It "was" unbelievable. And when he accused her of being jealous and spying on him, she had nothing to say.

"You are losing your mind. No one would believe what you are saying," he shouted in a degrading tone of voice. "You are seeing and imagining things."

Even to her, it was hard to understand. For months after that she asked herself, *I was tolerating all that violence. And now he is cheating? Why? Why?*

There was no answer at the time. Besides, she knew all too well that she would tolerate "this" too, as long as she could. She had a "very good" reason to not seek a divorce. A hurtful one.

CHAPTER 7
What Love Is

There are many definitions of the word 'love.' Sometimes some of us tend to confuse a strong desire or an unknown emotion with being in love. I think love is a divine gift, destined for those chosen to be blessed. It binds us, and leaves us powerless prisoners of its beauty until our last day. And I believe only those who have experienced it can really know what love is.

In the midst of the chaos surrounding her life she fell in love with her boss. It was unwilling, and unexpected as it always is. Suddenly, she found herself wandering through the most beautiful garden of emotions she had never experienced before. It was only then that she realized she had never been in love with her husband. So it is when we truly fall in love. We know it. We don't need to wonder, nor do we question why.

Maybe it was time to end her suffering, time for her to let go. Maybe that was the only way she would opt to get out of the hell she was living in.

For months, she buried her feelings. Despite all the problems she had with her husband, an extramarital affair was against her beliefs. She came from a good family, descendants of the last Russian Czar. She had been raised under Persian wisdom, and she believed in it. What she had heard so often from her mother was not something she could easily disregard:

"There is only one man for every woman."

"Your marriage should last until your final day."

"You remain faithful to your husband, for your children's sake, as long as you physically can."

Time passed. Now that she was aware of him being with another woman, his absences, which lasted longer each time, had become even more tormenting.

If only he'd ask me to forgive him, she often thought. But it never came. And as for her asking him for a divorce, he had only one answer: "I'll kill you instead. If we divorce, you are not going to see the children, ever."

"That" was not an empty threat. In Iran the children automatically belonged to their father at the time of divorce. It was extremely rare that a mother could get the divorce and custody of her children. And in the seventies in Iran a divorced woman was considered an indecent person.

It was in this unstable state of mind that she was drawn to her boss by the vigor of love. In her dark, helpless, lonely world, just a slight push could break her down. And the push came through a fallen angel, dressed as a friend. One, who later played a damaging, yet, in a way, helpful role in her life.

Suzy was a co-worker from another department. They met in the canteen and soon became friends. She was a widow in her forties, who had two children from her first husband. She was later married to an old rich man for his money. She was a sex maniac and, as it came out later, she had no respect for moral issues.

Although Iran was a modern country, Iranians' virtues are the aftermath of three thousand years of Persian culture. Personal attitudes, however, reflect the family background and individuals as they do everywhere -- so in the eyes of the majority who believe in strict moral values, a married woman's affair is immoral for whatever reason.

Suzy -- her colleague -- was a good listener, and the best that could happen to a person like her consumed by crises, as she was. They became friends within a short time. They met each other's families. And soon the two families were spending most of their free time and vacations together.

After a long while, they became good friends. She felt she could trust Suzy and confided in her about her husband's way of treating her and his betrayal. And shortly after that she admitted to her own 'sinful feeling' of love for another man.

Her friend, who was raised and saw things differently and now knew of the crisis in this young woman's life, tried to convince her to give up those 'old fashioned ideas,' as she called them.

"Don't be stupid, go for it," she'd say. "He hasn't been a good husband for you ever since you got married. Your life is ruined. And your husband is unfaithful to you. Why are you rejecting the one chance in your life to taste what love is?"

Still, she resisted temptation until the day that her husband rushed in suddenly and packed his belongings and left, never to return. This was the first time that he was leaving with suitcases.

When the rotten cord that had held her marriage together finally tore apart, she fell. Her suppressed emotions surfaced and she gave in.

On their first date, Fardad told her that he was married. He loved his wife of ten years and had been faithful to her throughout. Neither of them could explain or justify what was happening to them. But could anyone? Can we choose? Or set conditions for loving? No, there is nothing like "unconditional love." Because "love" doesn't set conditions to begin with.

She took him the way he was and cherished having him and all the beautiful feelings he brought out in her. She respected his love for his wife and his marriage, and adored him for it. She immersed herself in him, and loved him without reservation. And never, in the smallest hidden part of her heart did she wish him to leave his wife. It was just the way he wanted it.

He had the same feelings for her. He supported her and loved her, whichever way that *she* chose. His love for her knew no bounds. It led her to discover all the pleasant secrets of womanhood. It let her relish the wonderful taste of being a woman. A beautiful woman. A desired woman. A woman in love.

She learned for the first time, what being in love truly meant; needing someone so badly for no reason at all; that killing desire to feel his skin against hers. The feeling of weightless dancing in the air; like the lost feathers of young sparrows, floating in the spring breeze, while they mate on the trees.

Six wonderful months passed quickly. Then, her husband found out. And he turned it to the "only" happy period of her life. He had been gone for almost a year by then. How he did, was a shock and mystery to her.

One day he caught her alone on the street, in front of the office and played a dreadful scene. He started shouting: "I know what you have been doing while I was away. I have asked everyone who knows you to find out. Including the girls in the office, one of which is your friend, Suzy." She could not believe her ears. He went on, "I played such an impressive role as a dishonored husband, that Suzy felt for me and told me everything she knew."

He was swearing loudly, walking one step behind her as she headed to the car park. There, he hit her, kicked, and punched her, till she turned into a blood drenched baseball. And left, threatening to kill her if she went on seeing "that bastard."

However, it would soon become clear to her that he was lying all along about his way of knowing. It was not as harmless as he pretended to be.

Two days later he returned home as unexpected as he had left, not to make peace, but to destroy her soul up to the last piece.

She was putting Moosh and Roy to bed when she heard his heavy steps coming up the stairs. She quickly gave them a kiss goodnight, closed their bedroom door and ran into the other room. Expecting a scandal, she didn't want the children to hear or see it.

Seconds later he burst into the room, "I'm back. Don't you stand there with your back to me." He shouted.

She didn't answer, didn't even look his way.

He leaped towards her, took her by the shoulders and turned her around, "I told you I am back, aren't you happy to have me? Answer me."

She knotted her arms to keep her distance, trying not to look at his face, still didn't answer. She didn't know what to say. He was so unpredictable and violent, whatever she'd have dared to say would have been wrong. All she could say was whispering, "Just talk quietly, the children are sleeping." And that was enough to make him explode.

"They are more important to you than me, isn't it? Everyone is, even that married bastard. I should have killed you long ago." Then, he threw her on the floor. She quickly sat up, crouched herself and managed to lean against the wall with her back, to shield against another attack.

"I am listening to what you have to say, if you talk calmly," she whispered, looking at the floor. Then, he took a chair, put it by her knees, sat himself on the chair, and began, "I have an exciting story to tell. You're going to love to hear it." At that moment, she caught a glimpse of the sadistic expression on his face, it sent shudders deep into the core of her bones. She quickly turned her eyes away.

He made her listen in detail about his own latest adventure. And how he "really" found out about her from Suzy. And so the mystery was solved for her.

It went back much further to the day when she introduced Suzy to him at home for the first time. They had immediately become lovers. And they carried on all through the time when she and Suzy were supposedly friends. The day he left home so suddenly, he had moved into a flat with Suzy.

Even thinking about it was gruesome. *All the time Suzy was encouraging me to see Fardad, she had something else in mind.*

Her "best friend" had been her husband's agent from the very beginning. Suzy had been listening to her every word in the office and telling him everything while they were together. Mostly even exaggerated versions, according to what he was explaining.

But their relationship had not stayed the way *he* wanted. Suzy wasn't satisfied being a mistress. She wanted him to marry her. So as soon as he moved in with her, she began persuading him to get a divorce. She, too, would divorce her aged husband she promised. After a year of living together, Suzy finally realized that he had no intention of getting a divorce. So their sweet courtship turned sour and she moved out.

It was then that he came back to her like a wounded bear, to seek revenge. As she was listening to him, speechless, she remembered the day he stopped her in front of the office. He said: "Suzy told me of your affair, for she couldn't stand to see you deceiving me like this! She is a decent woman, not a whore like you! You should look up to her as a friend!"

Isn't Suzy doing the same to her faithful husband? She was thinking. *Is this the idea of a decent woman he is talking about?* It was sickening, the way Suzy had misused her trust and betrayed their friendship. *And now "I" am the one threatened to be killed?*

But with every word he said her ego melted a little, like a candle burning into tears. She couldn't even find the strength to blame either one of them. Or confront him. At some point she felt so exhausted she wished he "would" kill her, and free her from all that pain. *But what would my children do without me?* Her only thought was.

She heard him talking again, "I'd like to give you one last chance. I forgive you! I'll rent a place for us, if you'd give up work."

"Whatever," she said. "I thought if either of us had to do the forgiving, it would be me," she continued not expecting a response. "I really don't care anymore, and still don't understand what you want me for. Why not divorce? And why do you insist in I quitting my job?" But she might as well have been talking to the walls.

His threats were not empty. In those days a man, however ill-mannered himself, could kill his 'sinful' wife and get away with it. So she kept a low profile. And promised to stop her relationship. Which she did. In exchange, he rented a flat so they could start over.

At this point in time, she also agreed to give up working. She was feeling guilty despite everything he had done to her and was still hopeful of making her marriage work. *Maybe he has learned his lesson,* she thought for the hundredth time.

She quit, and they moved into a nice little house. He was calm for a few months, but he soon became bored. He could no-longer spend time with his friends. For that he needed more money.

So he began nagging her to get help from her mother. And to pressure her, he began using their budget to spend on his friends. More every day. She didn't know who those friends were, and if he was still seeing his cousin or Suzy. But she had to cope with all that. The only thing she was not ready to do was ask her mother for financial help.

Six months passed, and finally he realized that his plan had not worked, and she had no intention of asking for financial help again, even if he leaves her and the children with very little to live on. Until one day she warned him that she needed money to live, if he won't provide for them she would either go back to work or file for a divorce. At that moment he went crazy. He rushed into the kitchen, got hold of a knife and charged at her. She ran away; hiding in one bedroom, and then the other as he found her. Finally she escaped to the back yard, running around the flower-beds while he was following her, holding the knife above his head.

"You bitch. I should have killed you in the first place," he was shouting.

Moosh and Roy ran into the back yard, standing in front of their mother asking him to stop. "Please don't hurt Mom ... please don't ... please Dad." They were both crying and screaming. He didn't pay attention to them and went on.

"I shouldn't have given you a chance to live and make me so miserable. I am not going to do that again. You deserve to die."

Moosh and Roy ran to him hanging on his knees, so he couldn't move toward her. There, he kicked them away and threw the knife on the floor. When he saw them picking up the knife and bringing it to their mother, he stormed out of the house.

Ultimately she gave up. She could no longer subject her children to this kind of life. Until then she had tried hard to hide the truth from them, not let them see their fights. They sometimes heard them though, but that was unavoidable. So, soon after that incident, she finally filed for a divorce and prepared herself for another huge battle.

It started the day the notice arrived for him to appear in court. He came home around one in the morning. The children were asleep, and she was hiding in their bedroom with the door locked, expecting what was going to come.

When she heard him screaming, she knew he had seen the notice. She had put it on the kitchen table. She could hear the noise of things crashing on the floor and breaking. He wiped out everything on the kitchen counter, yelling, "How dare you file for divorce!" He opened every drawer, looking for a knife or any sharp object. She had hidden them all, knowing he would go for them. "I'll kill you! You sinful bitch!"

After a short while he approached the bedroom. He was punching and kicking the door. "Open the door or I'll break it. I am not giving you the freedom to go back to that bastard."

Inside she was shaking and praying. She wasn't sure how she was going to survive the night. Her Moosh woke up crying. He was pushing against the door, screaming like a maniac. Seconds later, as the lock on the door nearly gave up, she realized she had to do something. So she pressed all her weight against the door, then she opened it with a quick move. He stumbled forward, and fell flat on the floor. She used the chance and ran out of the bedroom, and out of the house.

It was after midnight. Barefoot in her pajamas, she headed for the police station nearby. A few minutes later she was there. She walked in and cried, "My husband is going to kill me! Please help."

The officer behind the desk gave her an absurd look. "Where do you live?" She gave him the address. He nodded, "I am sorry. Your house is out of our jurisdiction. I can't do anything for you. You have to go to the station at, ...," giving her the address.

She could not believe her ears. "Look, that is too far away from here. I can't get there without a car. I've come here on foot."

"Sorry, madam, but as I said we can't do anything for you," the officer answered.

"I am not going to leave until somebody helps me," she protested.

"You heard me madam. You can do as you wish," the officer answered, without taking his eyes off the paperwork in front of him.

She just stood there looking at him stunned, as if struck by lightening. He didn't even move his eyes. Agonized, she then took two slow steps backwards and slid down, as her back touched the wall. On the floor, she crouched, wrapped her hands around her knees, her head down and began crying.

Time passed. No one paid attention to her. The officers were moving around, doing their jobs as if she didn't exist.

Sometime later they changed shifts. She was still sitting there, hiding her face on her knotted arms, sobbing quietly. The new person in charge noticed her, and asked what she was doing there. She told him the story. "He's going to kill me if I go back alone."

The officer took her by the hand, almost carrying her out of the station. "I'll find transportation for you. Please don't cry."

Outside they waited for a passing car. Not many were on the road at that time of the night. After a long while an ambulance appeared. The officer stopped the ambulance and asked the driver to take her to the next station. "Good luck, my girl. Hope you understand. We honestly could not have done anything for you. It is against the law," he said while helping her step into the ambulance.

When she got in, she looked at the car's clock. It was three-thirty in the morning. She knew now there was no use going to the next police station. A woman in her state would be handled like garbage. She thought of going to her mother's. But that wasn't a good idea either, ringing the bell and waking everyone up. So she told the driver, "Please drop me at my house." It was as if someone was pushing her to go home.

When she arrived, she found her Moosh and Roy standing in the hallway, crying. She grabbed them, "Where is your daddy?" They pointed to the open window, "He went out there."

He had fled out the window in fear of the police. She thanked God a million times for having made the decision to go back. What would have happened to them if she hadn't gone back home that night? She never dared to think about it.

CHAPTER 8
The Second Ending

The next morning she took her children to the park. She was so sorry, having put them through the ordeal of the previous night. She sat on a bench, watching them play cheerfully in the playground, thinking what she should do.

At this time, she was twenty-seven, her daughter was five and her son only two years old. She was feeling guilty. She hated herself for giving birth to these two little innocent creatures. And for having given them less than they deserved. *How selfish of me and how cruel.*

I was too young. I didn't know what I was doing. And Mom didn't help me. I was trapped, but still, it didn't have to turn out like this. Trying to see things from this perspective didn't help her feel better either.

"Mom are you crying?" The children approached her.

She became aware of her face wet with tears. She wiped them away quickly and said, "No dear, I am not crying. Why should I?"

The little Moosh gave her a disbelieving look, "I know why you are crying. Because Daddy hits you, and it hurts."

She leaned forward, lifted her little treasure and sat her on her lap, "Yes, you are right. It hurts."

Her little girl exclaimed astounded, "Why don't we move to grandma's? If he is hurting you this way...!?"

Moosh's words echoed in her head forever, and they still do today. She suddenly realized that she was going down the wrong path for the second time. She felt stupid. It was no use hanging on anymore, for the children's sake. She gave her little Moosh a kiss on the cheek and said, "Well, we will. We will go back to grandma. I promise."

She decided right then to make it through the divorce no matter how difficult her life would become.

After her first failed attempt, she had realized that it was not going to be an easy task. She had to use the right tactic. One that would work without her being beaten or even killed.

I would begin by doing everything he wants, obeying him like a slave. Then, when the time comes, when I have his reliance however long it should take, I would cautiously ask him for a "temporary" separation, with the excuse that both of us need time to think things over. She thought she would say, *we would have time to forgive each other and start anew.* And, so that "he" wouldn't evade the court appearance, she planned to make "him" file for the divorce.

As unbelievable as it might sound her plan worked. It took great effort and patience on her part, but she did it. He was so arrogant, relying on his physical power and charm to get what he wanted. He happily thought he'd finally made her come to her senses. It never crossed his mind that he could be tricked by a mere woman.

It took a year for her to complete her plot. Ultimately he fell for her trick and filed for a divorce, which he had no doubt was only temporary. He was so full of himself and so selfish that according to him there was no reason why she would want to leave him for good. She knew him well by then, and used his own character to defeat him.

Shortly after, when he faced the true possibility of losing her, it hit him. By the time the court notice arrived for "her," he had figured it out. But it was too late.

At that point, to break her down he came up with the most vicious vengeance possible. He had to cause her such angst that she wouldn't dare appear in court. He did it on a weekend, one month after he had filed the divorce papers.

That day he looked thoughtful and sullen. As the four of them were having lunch, he first asked her if she had heard anything from the court. "Yes," she answered calmly, keeping an impassive face.

"But the date is not for two months." He remained quiet while they ate. After lunch he said he would take Roy for a ride.

"Don't you want to take Moosh with you?" She asked, surprised.

"No." His answer was short and abrupt. So she didn't insist.

When they left, she led her sad little girl to the bedroom where they took a nap together. It was early evening when they woke up. Roy and her husband weren't back yet. When the night turned late and they still didn't return, she became uneasy. Something was wrong. She could sense it.

She was right. They didn't come back. Not that day. Or any day. He had kidnapped their son.

Frantically she called his mother, his two married sisters, and anyone she could think of. But no-one knew where he was, or so they said. He had disappeared from the face of the Earth. Even at his work place he wasn't to be found when she called the next day. And the next. Day after day.

She knew she shouldn't go to the police or use force to find them. Because then, he would turn violent and that would jeopardize the divorce. For the same reason she asked her own family to stay out of it. To Moosh, who was asking constantly where her brother was, she said, "He'll be back soon." It wasn't easy, but she had to remain calm and act wisely.

The place that was supposed to be her home had turned into a chamber of torture, where she saw Roy wherever she looked. And heard his voice in every corner. So one week later, after her futile attempts searching for them had come to a standstill, she felt she could no longer live in the house without Roy. So one day--the day she was invited to attend her youngest sister's wedding--she packed, took Moosh's hand, and left for her mother's house.

The taxi stopped by the main entrance to the building. It was midmorning. She had aimed to arrive early, so as not to disturb the preparations. It looked like an extensive full traditional wedding. The garden gate was wide open. Long lines of helpers were carrying fruits, sweets, extra furniture and the wedding cake into the house. *Good for her*, she thought.

But for a few moments, they remained seated in the taxi and watched the commotion. It was a bizarre picture. The gate was open to celebrate her youngest sister's new life. And by the building's entrance, "she" was returning to get the divorce, with her daughter and only two small suitcases. *Just a few yards between the two doors, and a whole world of contrast,* she thought. *A beginning and an ending at the same time, in the same place for the same family.*

"Madam, I think this is your destination," the driver's voice brought her to the moment. He had put their suitcases out, waiting.

"Mom let's go," Moosh said.

"Let's go dear."

She noticed her mother standing by the garden gate, instructing the helpers. She waved as she saw them getting out of the taxi, and pointed to the door. Her hand gesture didn't say "welcome." It said: *"Get inside before people notice you."*

To the Persians, divorce is "immoral." And there is no exception. That was why she wasn't included in the preparations for her sister's wedding, as much as she wished she would. She was merely "invited" to the ceremony like any other guest.

When she got upstairs to her empty old bedroom, a radio was on. An old song was playing whose singer she did not know:

"When I was just a little girl
I asked my mother, what will I be
Will I be pretty? will I be rich?
Here's what she said to me:
Que sera sera, what ever will be will be
the future's not ours to see
Que sera sera, what will be, will be."

At the end of that long day her youngest sister left home. They were driven directly to the airport in her wedding dress and flew to Esfahan where her husband lived and worked.

It was a strange feeling. She didn't know much about her sisters, for she had been so deeply involved with her own complicated life.

But she still loved them very much. All three of them loved each other dearly, and nothing could take away from them their beautiful childhood memories. Even longer than childhood, in fact until she met her husband, they had been one soul in three bodies. And they still were, although their bodies were far apart.

The months between her arrival, going back to work, and the court date was one of the worst times of her life. Her heart bled each time she asked herself where Roy was and how he was. It felt as if her skin shrunk, pressuring her body, suffocating her. And her soul left her body a little bit each time she faced a closed door looking for her son. Even the air was not worth breathing without him.

The torture she endured during this time is not something anyone could identify with. Storms of ache poured nonstop and pierced her heart like acid rain leaving sore holes with each drop. They destroyed her from within. But on the outside she was a calm working mother with two children, and she was going to rescue them.

It was during this period that she learned how to shut off her thoughts in order to guard against pain. She learned how to consciously control her mind and deny the hurt. So she managed to reject all discouraging thoughts and fears. Even years later she couldn't remember much about that time, as hard as she tried.

This self-revealed ability gave her the tools, and her faith and her father gave her the power to survive. They never let her down.

Months later, on the first of September 1974, the date came for her to appear in court. Oddly enough, it was also her daughter's first school day. In Iran, children normally start grade school after their sixth birthday.

She dressed her beloved Moosh, tied her beautiful long black hair into two pretty ponytails behind her ears, and took her to school. Moosh was as brave as she was. She had missed her brother tremendously ever since, but she had never given her mom a hard time. Now, she was going to school and on her first day she behaved like a little lady.

When they arrived, she promised Moosh that she would bring her brother back soon. Then she gave her a long kiss and hug, told her how proud she was of her. She asked her to be a good girl. Then she left her to go to court.

Her husband was there when she arrived. She took a deep breath of relief. Then, she threw herself on a chair, so that the burden of that day's task wouldn't buckle her knees causing her to fall onto the floor. To him, she pretended nothing had happened, said a friendly hello, and asked how he was.

He looked dubious and a bit puzzled. So she gave him a warm smile to get him going. She had to play it just right. The children were all she had to fight for. She didn't want anything else from him.

The judge arrived and took his seat. He was in his sixties, pale faced and all-white hair. He looked humble and kind, and reminded her of her father. That made her win back her self-confidence. He talked for at least half an hour. She didn't hear anything at all until he stopped and turned to her, waiting.

"Sorry, what was it?" She said, almost jumping out of her seat.

"I said, you mentioned that you want the children. Is that your wish?" She could not remember having said anything. "Yes sir," she nodded.

"Where are the children now?" The judge asked her.

"My daughter is with me, and we live with my mother. My son is with him." She was careful with the words she used, not to sound critical or threatening.

The judge turned to him and asked if he was all right with that. He said, "I don't have any money to pay for her or the children's keep," instead of answering the judge's question.

"I don't want anything. No money. Just the children," she interrupted.

The judge gave her a hard look. "My girl, you must be mad," he said. "You are still young. You can remarry and have more children. If he doesn't want to pay, let him keep his children."

The discussion was going in the wrong direction when she heard her husband say, "Well then, I'll keep them."

So, she turned to the judge and said, "Please sir, I work and have some savings. I don't need money. I just want my children."

But the judge did not agree to that. "Look my dear," he said, "I *have* to mention alimony and child support in the divorce order. It's the law." He paused a few seconds, then added, "Unless you two want to go home and agree to something. In which case..."

She felt as if her life was running out. If we leave this room, she thought, I'll have to start all over again.

"Okay, how much have you decided he has to pay?" She interrupted.

The judge answered: "According to your social class, 3000 Toman (Iranian currency, equal to 3,000 Dollar at the time.) per month."

Her husband stood up, "No way. I don't have that kind of money." He said, his voice rising as he went on. "I will keep the children."

It was time to act, the moment she had waited and prepared for. She approached the bench and handed the judge an envelope. She had been so certain that she'd be needing it, she had carefully prepared the contents, and kept it in her handbag.

The judge spent a few moments reading her letter. Then he turned to her, thoughtfully, and looked at her for a long while. He was shaking his head from side to side, as if to say, "Pity you," while writing something, without saying another word.

When he finished, he gave her a piece of paper. "Here, this is your temporary custody document," he said.

He then turned to her husband and ordered him to bring back her son immediately. He added, "The lady has confirmed and signed this letter saying that she has received child support from you through each child's eighteenth year, plus her alimony in one lump sum." And added: "Ask the almighty God to forgive you, for what you must have done to your wife." And then, he told them they could leave.

Her husband got up, smiling and happy over his financial victory, he ignored what he'd just heard from the judge. And then they both walked out of the court house.

It was early afternoon. The sun was shining, not too hot and not too cold. Exactly right. She was relieved, yet not sure how he would go about returning Roy. She couldn't trust him. He put his arms around hers and said, "Let's go for a drink. We must celebrate our divorce." She agreed. She had to obey, not make him angry until she had her son back.

"We are representing the company I work for at the exhibition center. Let's go there till I close the stand, then we'll go for a drink." She didn't say anything, just followed him into his car.

The exhibition center was a huge temporary structure made of tents. Located to the north of Teheran, situated in an unused part of an endless parcel of land, miles away from the main road. It was assembled for the trade show each year.

Half an hour later they arrived. From the parking area, it took them another thirty minutes walk to reach the space that his company had occupied.

There, he asked her to sit on a chair and wait for him, while he got busy doing paper work and making phone calls. Fifteen minutes later a young man approached. "Miss Rosy is here," he announced, and left.

He jumped up, "Wait here. I have to see Miss Rosy. I'll be right back." He rushed out, without waiting for her to respond.

She sat there waiting. She didn't feel like walking around or looking at any of the exhibits. When the sun finally started going down, she realized she had been sitting there for a very long time, lost in her thoughts. Two hours later the lights came on.

There was no electricity in a radius of many miles, so the center had its own generators. They turned on and off automatically at the beginning and the end of the show. She waited for him until midnight. He hadn't come back yet. Half an hour later the center was almost empty. The stands were being closed down. Most of the employees had already left. He still wasn't there.

The last person to leave, an apparent co-worker of his, asked her what she wanted to do. She told him that her husband would be coming to take her home. "I don't have my car here," she explained.

The man looked at her surprised, "Oh, he didn't tell you? He left with Miss Rosy hours ago."

"He did?" She asked, trying to hide her embarrassment.

"Yes," he answered apologetically. "Would you like a ride home? There is no public transport around here," he offered kindly.

"No thank you, I'll call somebody to pick me up. I appreciate your offer anyway." She said that knowing very well that she didn't have anyone to call. She preferred not to share her hurt dignity with a colleague of his, feeling as small as a needle point.

After he left, she went on, walking toward the parking area. It was almost empty. Just at that moment the generators turned off and it got pitch dark. She continued walking. Every now and then a passing car guided her by its headlights. Then, there was nothing; dark, dead still.

When she left the lot surrounding the exhibition area, where the ground had been leveled and compacted, she lost track of the temporary road. She looked at the sky, it was black, looking forlorn without its moon, with just a few stars. She went on walking across acres of uneven land, over clumps of dirt and broken rocks, in the absolute darkness that veiled that whole section of the city.

Wandering through that endless empty black cave, she fell into the holes, crashed into chunks of hardened soil on the bumpy ground, then got back up and kept walking, crying and asking loudly, "Why, why me?"

Just as she thought she would never make it, the lights from a part of the main road showed, in the far distance. So she headed that way.

Finally she reached the main road. There, she started waving trying to flag down a passing car. That was something a decent woman would never do in Iran. But at that moment, she didn't care about anything but getting home.

Minutes later a car stopped. When she got in the driver turned the inside light on, probably to see what she looked like and ask her how much she charged. "What has happened to you?" He asked curiously, as he saw her soiled face, awash in a stream of tears. He offered her a box of Kleenex. "Do you want me to drive you to the police station?"

Under the dim inside light of the car, she became aware of her appearance. She had lost her shoes. Her nylon tights were in shreds. She was bleeding in several places on her hands, knees and feet. Her dress was torn to pieces, and the pieces were soiled.

"Oh, no, not the police station, thank you," she answered, terrified, while trying to clean up the dirt off her dress. "Just the bus stop or taxi stand would be a great help."

"You can't get on the bus in this shape. Do you want me to drive you to your destination?" She didn't turn to him to avoid making eye contact. He sounded truly concerned. So she felt comfortable enough to give him her address, thanking him for his help.

She entered the house quietly. It was long after midnight. And there was no noise, no lights. She went straight up to her bedroom. There, she let herself fall on the couch, weeping, without turning the lights on.

Five minutes later her mother, who knew she had been at court that day, opened the door. "Well, what took you so long? What are you crying in the dark for? Feeling sorry for yourself? It's all your own fault."

She said it all in one breath, standing in the doorway. Then she slammed the door closed and disappeared.

And so it finished, the day of the second ending of her life.

PART IV
ABANDONED IN AUSTRIA

CHAPTER 9
Escape from Iran

On a warm day in the early summer of 1978, they left Iran. She was thirty-two then, and from that day on her journey continued in the company of her two children for years and years to come. She said good-bye to her sisters, and her brother who had since married. Her mother was quietly crying the whole day, rarely coming out of the kitchen. Her youngest sister packed their three suitcases for them. She was there, but her mind and her thoughts were absent. She had shut her feelings off, as she had learned to do during bad times.

The first thing she clearly heard was the announcement of the flight attendant: "Ladies and gentlemen, this is the flight number 909 to Graz, Austria. Welcome aboard." How they had gotten there, she couldn't remember.

She was full of hope to make it, but didn't know how. Her children were sitting on either side of her. They were remarkably supportive. She felt so lucky. Her daughter was ten, and her son was seven years old. Considering the turn of events, they were taking it all with grace.

When the aircraft reached cruising level, and she lost sight of everything below, she lay back and gave in to her exhaustion.

She had not taken much luggage. The only important things she was carrying were some memories, their identity papers, and a few objects of emotional value. And the letters she had written to her daughter.

She took them out and started reading, to bridge the time during the long flight. She read:

My dear Moosh,

These letters should answer any questions you might have in the future. I'm writing them now, but will let you read them one day much later in life when you are a grown up and have your own children. Because "then" you will better understand.

So much happened to me before the divorce. But this is irrelevant. I don't intend to justify myself. I don't think I need to. Because what drove me to divorce, I am sad to say, you probably will remember for the rest of your life.

In fact, it was you who opened my eyes one day when you asked me why I didn't go back to Grandma's, if Daddy was hurting me. Your words let me see beneath that quiet, obedient, and lovely little face of yours. There was a girl who was suffering silently. And I was holding on just for you. What a blessing. I am so grateful that dear God made me see through what I was looking at.

My dearest; an eternal surge of love and energy was born in me in that moment when I gave birth to you. I will do anything humanly possible now to make it up to you and Roy for those unhappy years of your lives.

From now on, I will be in full control of my life. It will be devoted only to you and your brother. I won't consider anyone's wishes or way of thinking, nor would I ask for advice. I know what to do, and I am determined to do it. Let the whole world come against me for doing too much.

I'll do everything in my power to give you what a child deserves; in love, comfort, and friendship. I promise I will never let you feel that one parent is missing in our home. I'll give you more love than other children get from both parents. I promise.

Now read on, my dearest. I want you to know why we fled the country, leaving behind our homeland and all the precious people we loved so much. This is the entangled story of what drove us to escape from it all.

When we divorced, the court awarded me custody of you and Roy. You might remember the day Daddy brought back our little Roy. We both were so happy to see him, but I was heart-broken when I saw him. He had lost weight. He had a dingy shirt on, much too big for him. The shine of his skin was gone, as if he hadn't had a bath for a long time.

As he walked toward me, sucking his thumb, he had no shoes on. I'll never forget the desperate look in his anguished brown eyes, brimming with tears.

My dear, I shall raise you to be forgiving; for that's the way I am. But at that moment, when I saw my son that way, believe me when I say I turned to a ball of fire. I hated your father so much; I could have shot him there and then. Not only because of what he had done to my son, but also because I knew he had done that to hurt me. He had hurt you losing your brother, and Roy, keeping him away from us just to punish me. I don't know how long until I'll be able to forgive him, if ever, but I'll try my best.

Anyway, I was not receiving any money from him, so I went back to the university to pursue my education so I could provide a proper future for you and Roy. So I could offer you the quality of life that I had enjoyed when I was a little girl, with pride and dignity.

I was working at one place in the mornings and teaching at your school in the afternoon, remember? And then I was studying at night. It was a hard time for us, but the maid took good care of you. And Grandma was home in the early afternoon. Two years later, when I enrolled Roy at the same school, we were together during my teaching hours.

I got my engineering degree, and when I found a better job we had more time to spend together. Things were getting better for us. But I was still suffering. It never stopped.

From the day of the divorce, Daddy began to stalk me. He wanted me to go back, be with him again. When he found out that I was studying, he threatened me to take you away from me. I heard these words so often: "You are not spending enough time with the children. I don't need a court order. I'll take my children and go some place where nobody will find me."

He soon remarried, and I was pleased to hear it. But that didn't make a difference in him. "If you marry me again I will divorce her (his new wife). Otherwise, I'll take the children away from you." He used to say this each time he appeared in my way while watching my every move.

Can you imagine? He was being selfish and naive. He knew I would do anything to keep you. So, he tried to seduce his own children to get what he wanted.

His words were pounding in my head constantly. They were giving me the most gruesome nightmares; so bad, that I was terrified of sleeping. And yet, I was not going back to him.

At the beginning, you enjoyed being with your father. I had no intention of taking him away from you, or of letting you know what he was doing to me. But everything changed when he became a father again with his new wife. From then on he visited you in the company of his newborn son.

As you were both so young, I anticipated that you might grow to like his wife and their baby. If that had happened, I would have accepted it, and somehow dealt with the rest of my problems with him. But that didn't happen. Truly, things only got worse. With time, I learned that you couldn't accept sharing him with someone else. Each time he took you out, you both came back to me in tears. And I didn't know how to answer to your questions such as: "Does Daddy like his baby more than us?" Or "Why don't you please, please go with us when Daddy takes us to the park?"

The visitations had become a reoccurring ordeal for you two, and you needed me to support you. I understood your dilemma, but I couldn't become involved. If I had done that, he would have used you to get me back.

I begged him repeatedly to stop bringing his baby with him. But he wouldn't listen. He never did. He didn't have the caring eyes to see your heartache. I did, and I couldn't take it. So, the only way out of this misery was to get away from him, so far away that he couldn't reach us. That was when I planned to flee to Germany. Because you were born there, we could get a residency permit, and I would have been able to work. I worked long hours for two years and saved. When I attempted to get a passport for you, I was faced with the first setback. I was told that I needed your father's official permission to take you out of the country.

It was obvious that he wouldn't let me take you with me for good. So I had to lie to him. I told him that we were taking a brief vacation in Germany. He refused. We pulled and pushed for months before he gave me permission for a short trip.

Well, surprisingly, destiny is taking us to Austria now. The reason? Just before I bought our tickets, a very good family friend who had lived in Austria came to Iran for a visit. When I told him we were leaving for Germany, he asked me if I knew anyone out there, which I didn't. So he suggested that we go to Austria with him. He and his Austrian girl friend would help us settle down. It wasn't such a bad idea, much better than being in Germany, all alone.

We will be there soon. If everything goes well we will start a new life, a happy life, just the three of us, on each other's side, forever.

I have asked Grandma not to tell anybody where we are for now, especially Daddy. I hope I have done the right thing. I hope you will understand. And forgive me if you don't.

I love you more than the whole world.
Mom

She cautiously folded the letter and put it back in its envelope. Her daughter was looking out the window. She gazed at her lovely profile, and remembered the beauty of her long, black hair, that she had cut short in spite of her hefty protest. *I wish I could know what goes on in your little head at this moment.* Her Moosh didn't seem sad, but she was noticeably quiet.

With time she learned that her daughter had a complex nature.

She was reserved and extremely sensitive. It became a tough challenge to get through to her, or make her talk.

She turned to her son. Roy was asleep. She took the second letter and continued reading:

My daughter, dearest,

In springtime when it poured, when it thundered you and Roy rushed to me for comfort. I kept telling you that everything was all right. And hide my own fear of howling winds and thunderstorms.

But it's so extraordinary. When you are close to me, the warmth of your tiny bodies gives me comfort; it fills me with renewed strength and the energy to resist.

When I look around me these days, everything seems so unfamiliar. As if I no longer knows anybody here. Maybe it's because only one month is left before we leave. In my mind, I am already far away.

Here, no one accepts me as a decent person because I am divorced, for that is not condoned in this society. I constantly face indecent proposals from men.

Since your uncle, my brother, got married we had to make space for them, so we moved downstairs into the bedroom near Grandma's. I don't know, maybe I am wrong, but I feel I don't even belong in this house any more.

I feel an impulsive urge to run away from Iran. I can't clearly say why, but I have a feeling that more trouble is coming. Things could go very wrong in this part of the world. I told my sisters to get out too, but they don't take me seriously.

Sometimes I am scared, sometimes I am worried. It is the strain of too much responsibility. Sometimes I even cry. You haven't seen me crying! No. Because I cry in the shower, and let the running water wash away my tears. Grandma tells me to, "pray in the shower, and ask dear God for more patience." It works.

Early this year I had to take you to the hospital for an emergency tonsillectomy. All those painful hours sitting by your bed, looking at your angel face, I was praying that nothing would happen to you.

Shortly after that, it was Roy's turn. His handsome brown eyes were telling me that he was scared, going into the operating room. I carried him in, promising that the surgery would be painless and easy. It was as if a part of my body stayed in there with him. Inside, I was scared to death too. An easy surgery, yes, but so much could go wrong, God forbid. I knew, and that was what worried me.

When the door closed behind him, I sat outside, waiting. Oh, you don't know how much I needed somebody there, to hold and comfort me; to tell me that everything was all right. Someone to lean on. In those moments, I felt truly lonely without Grandma.

There have been so many times that I needed her, to complain about everything in the world. But she was always busy with everything else.

But I remember her faith, once during a forceful earthquake. That night the water in the pool was crashing wildly against the sides. We could see the splashing from the second floor balcony where we used to sleep in the summer. I was very young then. I remember I woke up. It was in the middle of the night, and my bed was rocking like a cradle. Grandma was sitting in her bed praying calmly, but loudly.

At first I was so very frightened. I heard my mother's voice praying, and then it was over. Her tender voice stirred me. Waves of peace converged on hearing her voice, and it inspired such strength in me. I remember telling myself I had no reason to panic -- she wasn't. So, I pulled the blanket back over my head and fell asleep.

I know I have learned a lot from her. Little things she does, things she says, they are engraved in my memory. I have learned to be brave, and rely on my own resources. I have learned to stay with God. "May this be an everlasting well of strength within you," she says.

You know, she hasn't been there for me much, and we don't get on well, but I have tried to learn from those elements in her that I admire, and she has plenty. "There is nothing you can't do, if you put your mind to it," she always says, and so it has been for me.

She encouraged me throughout, ever since I told her of my

intention to leave the country. The whole family was against it. A single mother with two small children in Europe? All on her own? She is mad.

But Grandma stood behind me, and promised to help us. Then, she said she wouldn't go to the airport to see us leave. That hurt me a great deal.

Well . . . I don't understand. Maybe this is her way of hiding her tears from me. You know, I have never seen Grandma cry ever.

I don't know when we will see her again after we leave. Grandma and I are so unlike, but I love her very much, and have never stopped needing her. I don't want to lose her. Unknowingly, she has been a strong source of moral support.

I hope to be a good teacher for you and Roy. If not much more. Wish me luck. I love you two more than anything in the world.

Love and kisses,
Mom

CHAPTER 10
Life by the Souvenirs of a Kingdom

The plane landed in Graz, Austria at dusk. The small arrival lounge was nearly empty. The only persons there were the arriving passengers and a few fatigued customs officials.

Reeling, they looked around for a place to sit down while the friend who had accompanied them to Austria waited for their luggage to arrive. They found a cold marble bench near the exit door. Devastated by the contrast between this place, and Teheran's lively airport; the sunny warm day they had left, and this freezing cold, all three of them were shivering like newborn kittens.

Sometime later the friend finally appeared with their luggage. "Lets go, my girlfriend's brother is waiting for us outside," he said, walking past them toward the door. They followed him. "My girlfriend and I don't live together. You'll be staying with her for the time being," he explained as he walked ahead.

In the car, the young mother still couldn't imagine what to expect. She only knew of "a girlfriend," and that was all. To her, everything seemed like a bad dream, gliding across the land of obscurity in slow motion. *What will be, will be*, she told herself, putting her arms around her children and pressed them tightly to her chest.

The brother who was driving, was a tall young man with blue eyes and blond hair. He had a heavy sheep-skin jacket on and jeans. Clean but not so elegant. He spoke with a strong suburban Austrian accent. He was hard to understand. His sister and he were descendants of a noble Austrian family. His sister (the girlfriend) lived in the family castle in a small village on the Yugoslavian border. This was as much as she knew about them.

They finally arrived. It was dark and foggy, and she couldn't see much. In the small light area in front of the car she just saw a gate without doors. They drove through, turned left and stopped near some wide stairs. The stairs led to the entrance.

A young chubby girl opened the door, introduced herself and let them in. She was Monika, the girlfriend, who was trying to sound very friendly. But she didn't manage well. They followed her into a long, half-dark hallway walking on the creaking wooden floor that felt as if it would crumble under their feet at any moment. At the end of the hallway they reached a high and heavy-looking door on their right. She stopped, and so did they.

It was an old wooden, double door used as insulation against cold and noise. The first door opened outward, the second one, which stood about ten inches back, squeaked and opened inward. Then they were led into a very large right-angled room. It was damp and warm, but felt strangely cold. An unsavory smell of food filled the air. The place was a kitchen-living room. It was so poorly lit that it took them several minutes to notice that there were only a few pieces of furniture in there.

On the right wall there was a wood stove, and the steam that filled the room was coming from the two cast-iron pots on the stove. Like a fireplace, but standing near the wall, it was probably the first invention after the age of open-fire cooking. They called it 'kachelofen.' It burned wood to heat up the stove. After the cooking was done, the glowing embers worked as a storage heater.

Dinner was served almost immediately. And after that, they got to hear the history of this awesome relic and its inhabitants.

The owners of the castle, which was around five-hundred years old at the time, were Monika's forefathers. They were dukes and duchesses, and the castle was a part of their large fortune. The last ones who lived there, during the Austrian monarchy, had been Monika's parents.

She told sad stories about the time when Yugoslavia took over that part of Austria. "I remember hearing it, from my mother; one day we woke up in the morning and there was the new border, not far from the castle, our home."

"Overnight, our family was divided into Austrians and Yugoslavians. We lost most of our family members to Yugoslavia. And we never met again until sixteen years later, if I remember exactly, when the relationships between the two countries became normalized. I'll take you with me sometime, when I go over the border to visit my aunt. It is easier now. Especially for us who live in the border towns."

By the end of the first World War, when the Austrian kingdom was abolished, they had lost their entire fortune except for the castle. Monika then went on proudly to say that this remarkable dwelling was her birthplace. She had continued living there after her parents died. The old building was a landmark now, but she still was the proud owner.

The room they were having dinner in was now the only part of the enormous building she occupied. She had a bedroom with a bath behind the door on the left wall. The rest of that part of the building was abandoned. She had rented a couple of the rooms in the north wing to the farmers. That was her income.

The newcomers were to live in the castle until they found a place of their own. They became used to it after a while, but the first night they experienced the most horrifying adventure of their lives.

When bed-time came, the girlfriend asked them to follow her to their room. Out of the living room, she got hold of a lantern, and lit it. Then she turned right, and they followed her up a narrow wooden stairway. At the end of the steps, they reached the second floor verandah. Immediately, she stopped. There was a heavy wooden door on her left, she opened it and went inside. After turning the light on, she stepped to the left, now holding the lantern by her face, and let them in.

The smell of dead air and humid dust drifted out and they found themselves in a spacious room with no windows. The only lighting came from a small wall light by the door. Large portraits with massive frames hung on the four walls. Numerous tall and short statues were standing on the left side of the room by the opposite wall, covered with white linen. They occupied most of the left part of the room as if stored there, gathered from all over the place. In front of them a large antique king-size bed, its headboard to the right. So that lying in bed, the statues were in full view. A few yards behind the headboard was a fireplace with a generous opening. And a huge antique piano, hidden under hundreds of years of dust, stood next to the fireplace.

They put their suitcases on the bare floor. "Let's go, I'll show you the bathroom," their hostess said and walked out the door.

They followed her in absolute silence. Out on the verandah, she turned right and put the lantern on the first step of a much narrower stairway. It led up to the rooftop. "That is the bathroom there," she said pointing up with her thumb without looking that way.

They could barely see the shadow of a tiny shed. "Take this lamp with you when you go up there. There is no electricity," she added in a rush and charged down the stairs.

So they went back to the room. She quickly took pajamas out, to put the children to bed before the gloominess of the place soured their mood. They changed, turned the light off, and looked for the bed in the dark.

She placed her children on either side of her, with her arms under their heads. She knew they were frightened, even though they were trying to be brave. She hugged them and assured them that she would stay awake, and wait for them to go to sleep first.

The room did look spooky. The wind that was blowing down the wide chimney made a shrill noise behind the bed. She tried not to move as the children dozed off.

Half an hour later she heard her daughter say, "Mom are you sleeping?" The little girl was restless and needed to make sure that Mom was still there for her.

"No, I'll wait for you to go to sleep," she reassured her and pressed her Moosh tighter to her chest.

While she was waiting for her children to fall asleep, she looked around. It was nasty. The white covered statues looked like ghosts standing still, waiting for midnight to start wandering around.

At the midnight hour she was wide awake, praying. Her heart was beating in a frenzy. She was trying to convince herself that the movements she saw were only caused by the draft, blowing in from the fireplace, making the linen covers ripple.

When she finally heard Moosh and Roy's regular breathing, she closed her eyes. None of that experience had shaken her faith, and nothing in the world could bother her when she was with her children. In spite of the "ghosts," she fell asleep instantly.

Early the next morning she saw the first daytime view of the area, from the small window in the shed, called the "bathroom." It looked like a picture hanging on the wall; a picture that etched itself in her memory and remained forever.

She was looking down. The castle seemed to have been built on an elevated platform, midway up a very high mountain. She could see endless rows of aged pine trees below. They covered the slope down to the valley and up to the next hill.

From that point on, she could see nothing. The picture was cut off by a milky background wall of dense fog that verged upon the sky. It overlaid the top of the trees, looking like a milky-colored hat of fog in the distance. As it stretched toward the window which she was standing behind, it became less dense and turned to a fine mist

When the children woke up, she took them for a walk before breakfast. They came down the narrow stairs and passed the living room.Now they could see that the long hallway was the first floor verandah. It had a series of doors on the left, the first of which opened to the living room. Each of those doors opened to one large room. From inside, they were connected to each other by more heavy doors. They looked like railroad wagons, only much bigger. It ended with the entrance door after the wall made a right corner. On the right-hand side of the verandah, there was a wall with big glass openings onto the courtyard. It enclosed the verandah up to the second floor.

They walked out of the building, turned right, and down the stairs into the courtyard. The yard was a north-south rectangle, surrounded by the building. A fountain in the shape of a flower was in the center of the yard, with a tall statue of a dancing girl in the middle. It looked old, fractured, and forgotten. A few inches of brown water covered the bottom of the fountain and some soaked dead leaves underneath it.

Some women and children, tenants of the north wing, opened their doors. They stood there watching them, stone-still, as if observing aliens from the moon. She ignored them.

They continued their expedition in the opposite direction, toward the south wing. The private chapel was on that side. It was well maintained and clean. Then they turned around, and walked to the east wing. That was where the stables used to be, and it still smelled like one. It was now used as a warehouse.

Next to the stables, they turned a corner of the building to reach the gate. They stood by the gate for a few moments, looking up and around. The facade of the ancient building spoke for itself, of the glory it had once experienced and of its age. It had a beige color, or perhaps white-gone-beige through the years. The paint was cracked and various spots were damaged with pieces missing.

Breakfast was served just like dinner, in a traditional, royal way. The table was packed with antique dishes, silver cutlery, embroidered fine cloth serviettes, and antique china containers, which held a variety of home-made marmalades. There were more expensive dishes and tableware on the table than food, most of which remained unused and unopened.

While they lived in the castle they faced culture shock in its most cruel style. Their hostess made constant efforts to impress them, having been acquainted with a Persian male, she had learned that Persians are well known for being excellent hostesses. But obviously she was going over the top to hide her bitterness for falling from the top of the monarchy to an ordinary farmer, which was not an issue to them as her guests.

Monika's constant efforts made life more difficult for her. Being a humble and down-to-earth person, she didn't look for glamour in life. So, to convey her appreciation for a place to live--which would have been common between Persians--she continuously pretended to be impressed. The whole charade sapped her energy.

She constantly searched Monika's face for signs of sincerity, but found none. Her acts were in total conflict with her words which claimed modesty. Luckily, they soon found a place in town. It was a three-bedroom furnished flat on the third floor of a residential building. It belonged to an old single lady, a distant family member of Monika, who was vacationing abroad. She welcomed the opportunity and rented the flat for the period that the lady was to be away.

They packed their three suitcases again, thanked their hostess candidly and left delighted, running away as far as they could from the moldy remains of the Austrian monarchy. They left behind the little village and its folk, who had been hanging on to their forefather's life-style for decades, and the monarchy that had been destroyed almost sixty years before then. And as far as she knows, they still are as the world prepares itself for the year 2000.

The first night in the new place was unfamiliar but easier. She put her children in one bedroom and she took the other one. The next morning a loud vibrating noise woke her up well into the day. The racket, which was shaking the flat, came from the road-side. She leaned out the window and saw an electric-tram passing just below, so near she could touch its roof.

The town, Graz, was a small university town. It was clean, and despite its old age, it was well kept and the landmarks restored and well maintained. People were extremely friendly. They smiled at you and tried to talk with you and help any way they could. The cost of living was much higher than in Iran at the time, but there were many ways to live on a low budget. Areas where she could find clothing and food for half price. Women didn't follow the latest fashion, but they were always properly dressed. Not extravagant, but clean and pleasant.

The public transport, trams and buses, were on time and reliable. And because of the city's small size, you could live there forever, without needing a car. It took one and half hours to travel by tram form one end of the city to the other.

Her next task was to find a school for the children. Their friend gave her some information about good areas and schools, and within a month they had reserved places for both Moosh and Roy. The only slight problem was that she couldn't place them together in one school. It meant more transportation costs, but she had no other choice. Two weeks later they found a nice one-bedroom, unfurnished flat on the third floor of a five-story building. It was in walking distance to Moosh's school.

The day they moved was a happy one. She used part of her savings to furnish the flat with basic necessities. Among them, a small short-wave radio and a black and white TV.

Then, they had the most wonderful time together decorating the flat and hanging their clothing in the wardrobe. The bedroom didn't have enough space for more than two beds. So she assigned it to the children. And she took the futon in the living-room to sleep on. They had cooking space in a set-back corner of the same room.

Cooking Persian food together and lunching together became great fun. They could find all the ingredients in the small market, only twenty minutes walk from the flat. That was when Moosh slowly learned to cook Persian food. Within a short time that small place looked like home and smelled like home. Where they had a piece to remind them of Iran in every corner.

During the two weeks they had left before school started, she took them to the park every day to give Moosh and Roy an opportunity to meet other children. Before long they made friends with the neighborhood kids, and soon they left her on her own. Then, she would sit on the small balcony of the flat and watch them as they played with the blue-eyed, blond Austrian children.

She had made her mind up to stay in Austria, and mixing with the local children was the best way for Moosh and Roy to learn the language. It was an opportunity to grow into competent and adaptable adults. For the same reason, despite them not knowing a single German word, she had signed them on at a local school, without wasting time for German classes.

Evenings, after she put them to bed, she would quietly go to the next room. There, she'd lay on the futon, and listen to music from an Iranian station on her short- wave radio. That little black box was her connection to her country and all the memories she had left behind.

She also found time for writing. She used to write short stories and poems before she got married. But the chaos of her married life had broken her peace of mind, and along with it her creativity.

On the fifth of September 1978, the school year started. Her children were ready for the unknown. She, on the other hand, was concerned and curious about their reaction. Especially on the first day. Starting at a new school is always a struggle for kids. In this case, they had to face a completely different culture without knowing much of the language.

She asked her Persian friend to take Moosh in for the orientation day while she dropped off her son. Roy, who was now eight, wasn't hesitant. And she pretended that everything was just fine. On the way back she went straight to the church.

There was a catholic church just opposite their building; its bells so close that she could see them in their true size behind the window. They used to ring every morning and evening. She loved the clang of those two enormous, heavy, metal bells, as they swung in opposite directions.

She went in and sat down at the feet of the Holy Mother. "I have come here to ask for your help. I am not a Christian, just a lonely mother in need of refuge, with no-one to turn to. I need to talk. You are a mother, you understand what I am going through. So please help me for your child's sake. Please help my children to maintain their tolerance and their courage. Please grant them the skills to survive. I am the only person they have in the whole world. Please save me from failing them."

Shortly after that day, when she was able to transfer her son to Moosh's school, she was certain that her prayers had been heard.

Time went by, and the children grew accustomed to their new environment. Their language limitations bothered them the least. They were growing up to be lively and happy children, and she was enjoying life with them to the fullest.

She would walk them to school every morning and pick them up in the early afternoon. In between, she kept house. Every month her mother sent them some money. It wasn't a lot, so she spent it sparingly, so as not to have to dip into what was left of her savings. And since she had been warned about Austria's severe winters, she got busy knitting woolen pullovers, hats and socks for the children, preparing for the long, cold season ahead. While knitting, she had more time to listen to Persian music, aired directly from Teheran on her short wave radio station.

CHAPTER 11
Revolution of Iran—Annihilation of an Era

On November 21st of that year, four months after they had left home, Roy turned eight years old. At home they had big parties for their birthdays, but this time it was only the three of them.

The quality of life, however, kept improving for her children. The first Christmas in Europe, they spent with a neighbor. A single mother whose daughter was Moosh's classmate. One week before that, the children had joined the school's Christmas party. They met Santa Claus for the first time. Not being Christians, they had never celebrated this joyful holiday. They were excited having taken part in a custom of the new culture and talked about it in detail for hours. By then, they could communicate with their peers more easily. Both of them had taken their places amongst the children at school and in the neighborhood.

Moosh turned eleven in January 1979, seven months after they had arrived in Austria. They celebrated her birthday in the company of three of her school-mates, but there were not many gifts for her as in the past.

She couldn't offer more than that to her children, as much as she wished to. Yet they never pestered her about the material things they couldn't have. Not a word of disagreement. Not a trace of disappointment or any sign of despair. Even though she knew well that they missed all that.

They had learned from her how to survive. She motivated and encouraged them throughout their worst of times not to give up. And they proved that she had made the right choice taking them with her. She too, learned from them. She learned that children could understand and be supportive if you are not too proud to admit needing their help, and they will if you talk to them in all honesty and help them understand the situation.

All three of them were settling in successfully until that fateful day in February 1979. A day that led to a turning point in the history of the world. The day that she would never forget

That freezing day in February began like any other. She picked up the children from school as usual, and while they were having dinner she turned on the radio, which as always was set on the voice of Iran's station. A program which was aired directly from Teheran for Iranians overseas. But instead of the normal program there was a live report from Teheran. She immediately became alert:

"The whole downtown area is burning. The revolutionary fighters are blocking the roads. They are preventing the fire trucks from getting close enough, to put the fire out. Oh my God they have put the fire engines in flames. They wouldn't let the driver get out. Oh... he is burning in the truck." Then he began shouting: *"Explosion ... explosion..."* she couldn't hear anything else, for his voice faded away in a terrifying sound of the explosions -- her world was being blown apart.

There was a short pause at that point. The speaker then said that he was waiting to be connected to another reporter, in a different part of the city. The first reporter on site was presumably dead. Shaking all over her body, she turned off the radio, took the children to the bedroom and asked them to stay there. Both of them had sensed that something was very wrong; without asking questions they remained in their room quietly.

Until she and children moved into their tiny one bedroom flat, she knew very little of the turmoil. She was preoccupied with plans for the future and adjusting to their new world. When they moved and

she bought the short-wave radio, she heard about the riots in scattered short news. According to the commentators, the seeds of the plot had been secretly planted years before.

It came into the open in the summer of 1978, shortly after she and the children left the country when violence erupted in the holy cities. The pro and contra government groups were attacking each other in the streets. No one expected it to last, for it had happened in the past, without many consequences. But this unrest, a religious movement, soon proved to be a larger and more organized movement than it first appeared.. The protests turned into riots. And the riots grew more fierce and more violent. Within a short time, the turmoil spread to other cities, and then to the capital city, Teheran, and soon the whole country was involved. As the overwhelming mass of angry citizens charged into the streets, the army's show of force was no longer able to ensure order. The fight between those for and against the government blew the peace apart.

After only a few months, on the 16th of January the Shah of Iran left. And on the 1st of February the revolution leader, Imam Khomeini, who had been living in exile in Paris, arrived at the Mehrabad Airport, Teheran's main airport.

Now it was Friday, February the 11th, 1979. The day that is called the 'Black Friday' in Iran. The day that Moslem activists prevailed and took command in Iran. It was a day that brought havoc to many lives, and an end to many more.

And for her, it was the day she lost her homeland as she remembered it. She lost her childhood, her youth, her friends. And all the places where she grew up. All the ties to the past thirty-three years of her life, and beyond, turned to smoke and dissolved in the toxic air. May be it was meant for her to be far away from home when it happened. But she could not escape hearing it in live reports on the radio. She experienced her loss unexpectedly, moment by moment, as it happened as the news echoed around the world.

She returned to the program. The terrible news continued. The bit she had heard before was coming from the south of the city, a compacted area in Teheran. When she joined again, the revolutionaries had advanced. They were now in the central parts of the city. To overthrow the regime, they had to reach the government seat located in the north, as well as the site of the main radio station which was broadcasting at that moment. That was also in the north of Teheran.

Ice cold blood ran through her veins. The north was where her mother and most of her immediate family lived. She didn't dare to think what might happen to them. All she could do was pray for their safety.

The broadcaster was reporting each incident as it occurred. He named the main buildings, the roads and the places that she knew. They were burning to ashes. According to him, the whole city had turned into a battlefield. Anyone who was around, innocent people who happened to be on the roads that day, they were all killed. Dead bodies covered the streets. And the army was nowhere near success.

The reporter continued: "The militants are approaching us in the north." Minutes later: "I can hear them now. Shootings, explosions. Our building is quaking. Oh God ... they are in the building now!"

His voice grew louder and louder. He sounded desperate: "I request back-up. The station is under attack. Brothers, soldiers, we need urgent help.... They are here! Please help us. .... Oh ... God, help me.... help...." And then there were some unrecognizable noises like falling objects, breaking glass, shots, and then silence. Dead silence.

"To all the citizens of Iran, this is the voice of the Revolutionary government, we hereby announce our victory."

With those words, the voice of home on her little black radio died forever.

By the time the cold winter set in, life had changed. She received no more letters from home, no telephone calls, and no news from any

radio or TV station. She even didn't know if her family was still alive. Since the revolutionaries had taken over, they hindered the spread of the news to the rest of the world. All means of contact to and from Iran were cut off. Her Teheran's short-wave radio station never went on the air again.

She kept the worst of the news from the children. But she did explain to them that the money from home had stopped, and she was under tremendous financial pressure. They were now living on her savings, so she couldn't afford more toys or entertainment for any of them. And if they were to survive in Austria she had to look for a job, and that could imply difficulties in their quiet life.

So she began searching straightaway. There were many positions advertised in the local newspapers, but most were low-paying, and ones that no Austrian would take. She applied for the better jobs first, but her attempts were all unsuccessful. She didn't mind; she lowered her sites to cleaning floors, toilets, washing dishes and baby-sitting. But she was turned down, one after another, week after week.

Now, every sunset, every rejection, came upon her like a beam of fire. But she wouldn't let disappointments get her down. Every night she took the holy book, Koran, and read and prayed.

She was only glad that no Persians in the area knew her yet. They would have despised her for seeking low-level work, and she would be cast out from the Persian community. The attitude was that an educated Persian who had worked in top places in Teheran should never stoop to menial labor. A member of her social class would rather go back home, than live with such an embarrassment.

But she did not care about those ideas. She had no intention of returning to Teheran and putting her children back into their father's hands. She still remembered what he once said after they divorced: "You can't survive without me, you'll come back and beg me for forgiveness." So she was set to take any job, to spare them that.

Weeks passed and still no one had hired her. Her savings were decreasing. It looked as if, despite all her efforts, things pointed in only one direction: back to Iran. But she wouldn't accept that or give up. Whenever she felt she was standing on the edge, she would go to church and ask the Holy Mother to rescue her.

Finally, one day help arrived. Ironically, it came through the children. For sometime she had noticed a black-haired boy playing with them in the back yard. She asked Moosh who he was. She told her that he was a Persian and lived next door. "They have lived here for a long time, and his father has many carpets!"

From Moosh's explanation she figured that the man must be a rug merchant. The next day she went knocking on their door. She was counting on the help of an established Persian family to find her a job.

A tall lady with short black hair, kind face, and perfect manners opened the door. She introduced herself to the woman, and told her that she lived in the next building. And explained that she was looking for a job because the situation in Iran had left them with almost nothing. She asked the lady if she knew of anyone who would need a worker in the house or anywhere. The lady was friendly and forthcoming, but she couldn't help.

"Come back in the evening and meet my husband. He might know of something." So she went back later in the evening, still hopeful.

The husband was a Persian architect. He imported Persian carpets on the side. They had been in Austria for over ten years. He mentioned that one of his friends was a famous Austrian architect. "I have worked with him for years. A very nice gentleman. He might need someone for his office. It's not too far from here. I'll talk to him and let you know." She thanked them and left.

A week later she received a telephone call: "He would like to meet with you. I can take you to him tomorrow, do you have time?" *What a question,* she thought.

"Let's see what you can do for ten trial days. Then I'll decide," the famous architect said after the interview. Two weeks later she started. The ten days turned into almost six years.

Her boss was the kindest human being she had ever met. A

tanned-skin, big-built gentleman in his forties. He must have had foreign blood in him, he had black hair, a black full moustache and green eyes. A strong character with a smile, that never ever left his face. Later he said, "When I met you, I was moved. You were a young single mother, trying to save your children. Considering the circumstances in Iran, I admired your courage. And just didn't have the heart to say no to you."

Her guardian angel had taken her by the arm once more and pulled her out of her misery. The architect, his wife and two children became good friends to her and her children. A caring big brother, and an aide to all three of them for as long as they lived in Austria. In fact, for as long as *he* lived. Because he kept in touch where ever they were. He even visited them years later when they lived in England. And two years after they left England, she received a letter from his wife saying that he had died of cancer.

Such a waste of humanity, she thought, when she sorrowfully learned of his premature death. "He was an angel. Maybe angels belong to the heavens."

CHAPTER 12
Something Old, Something New, Something Shiny was Untrue

Only a week passed before she encountered the next obstacle. She was not allowed to work in an office as she was told by the personnel department. Her boss guided her through the right channels. She would be able to work only if she was a student. To her, it was yet another challenge to overcome. Grateful for his advice, she turned to the Technical University in Graz, which was just behind the office. Luckily, the system worked for her.

In the admissions office she learned out that the higher education system in Austria was not on a yearly plan. That meant that the students would graduate after having passed a specific number of units regardless of the length of time they might need for finishing the course. Attending lectures was not compulsory, and especially in subjects like art and architecture, to learn the theory and practice simultaneously, students were expected to work during the course.

Another blessing was that international students from "Third World countries" didn't have to pay tuition. And Iran was regarded as such!

She submitted an application form attached to certificates of her prior education. It proved wise, having the papers translated into German, and taking them with her out of the country.

Her boss let her carry on working until she received a response from the university. During the waiting period she worked hard to earn as much as she could in case she was rejected and had to find work in the black market.

The children quickly learned the new routine. In the two weeks before she started, she showed them how to get to school on their own, which side of the road to take, and which side to come back on. She showed them where the safest spot was to cross the main road. Then she let them walk to school for a couple of days, and followed them a few yards behind to see how they did.

Years later when she thought about it she got chills. As they say, "If I knew then what I know now, I wouldn't have become what I am today."

She always remembered what her mother used to say: "You take the first step, and God will show you the rest of the way." And she wished to raise Moosh and Roy, to have the same attitude.

They arrived home from school in early afternoon, long before she got there. So she hung a house key on a cotton string and gave it to her daughter. She asked Moosh to carry it around her neck, and keep it underneath her dress so no one could see it.

She reminded them over and over again to behave wisely. She made them realize that she was doing this for them, and that she needed their help to make it work. She promoted their sense of awareness and responsibility. They understood, in spite of their tender age of eleven and nine. And somehow, it all came together.

Three weeks later she received a letter from the university. She was accepted. Overjoyed, she screamed, sang and danced. And hugged and thanked her children, while they watched her, perplexed, not knowing how important the letter was to her. And what she was thanking them for. The future was smiling at her again. And she felt it was all thanks to their support

She worked hard and her boss supported her like a father, but the other employees never accepted her as one of their own. They didn't like the fact that she had become the boss's favorite. She noticed, but didn't mind. She had a more important goal to achieve.

One of her co-workers was an English student. He was a shy, modest young man, her age, clean but sloppy. He didn't dress like she always imagined the English would do. And looked as if nothing in the world mattered to him. He was the only one who established a friendship with her. He was kind and caring to her. It was a rescue, so she didn't refuse his sympathy.

John had lived a wild life until then. Years of good time, many women, drinking, traveling. So he had not achieved much in life, and didn't seem to have any intention of getting to somewhere. After a short while, when they got closer, he told her that he was divorced and had a boy from his first marriage who lived with his ex-wife in Germany. He told her that he was tired of living that way and wished for a quiet family life with a decent wife.

To her, the most important issue was trusting him with her children. But she made it clear to him that she didn't love him and didn't intend to remarry.

The following summer months were difficult. She had to make arrangements for the children and couldn't afford a baby-sitter or summer camp. That meant they had to stay home during the time she worked. She explained it and told them that she didn't want them going out of the house while she was at work, for should something happen to them she wouldn't be there to help them. They understood and somehow accepted their confinement. That summer, their first anniversary of arriving in Austria, went by smoothly.

She used to call them every hour from work to check on them. They played together, watched TV, and were busy the whole day. On the weekends they had Saturdays for cleaning, shopping, laundry and ironing together. And Sundays they would go to the park, church, or sightseeing. They were enjoying life the way it was meant to be, in peace and harmony. All three were holding on to each other for better or for worse.

In September, 1979, the children were looking forward to going back to school. By then, their second school year in Austria, they had become well adjusted to their new way of life.

Six more peaceful months passed quickly. She worked, studied, and watched her children grow. They were doing well at school, and bravely withstood the days they had to walk to school in the freezing cold. They survived the second cold season with no major difficulties.

When the snow started to melt, the unbearable winter gave way to the rainy, cold spring. By the end of the school year, the warmer days had come.

Almost eighteen months had passed since the revolution, and she still couldn't get news about Iran. She had no idea what was going on there. The mail didn't function. And she hadn't heard from any of her relatives, or her ex-husband.

In May, she learned that telecommunications were finally restored, for she received the first phone call from Teheran. They were all right, but didn't give her much information about the situation. She knew very well why. That was the way her family was. Just like her, they would never spread bad news, so as to nourish each other's peace of mind. But she was joyous just to know they were alive.

That school holiday, 1980, was also going to be an exciting one for the children. Their grandma was coming to Austria for a visit. It also meant that things were working in Iran again and that air travel was now reinstated.

It was good to see her mother again. The children were thrilled. They toured the city and spent a busy and beautiful time with Grandma, while she worked. But for her, the reunion turned into a disaster. It began with Grandma's cold response to her passionate welcome at the airport. It said it all. Her mother was arrogant and reserved. It seemed as if to her mother, the fact that a daughter of her's was divorced meant she had a scarlet word on her forehead: rejection. And nothing else she did, mattered.

After two months, when Grandma left, they all cried. Her mother was everything to her in spite of all their differences. Seeing her leave so coldly, was devastating. She wished she could die, be born again, and live her life differently to win her mother's respect that she so longed for. It was obvious that her mother would never forgive her for her "unsuitable marriage." And facing the fact that she was not a forgiving person was beyond her strength.

The disappointment, however, not only didn't get her down, it made her try harder and achieve more. To prove herself to her mother, she subconsciously pushed so hard that she forgot herself. This made things better for her children, but not for herself. It turned to become her loss.

Under these circumstances her English colleague, found a chance to get involved with her. She was glad to have him as a friend. But in her heart, she couldn't find love or affection for him, as much as she searched.

Little by little he managed to spend more time at their place than in his flat. Finally, one night when he came for dinner, he didn't go back. Days, weeks and months passed, and he stayed with them in their tiny one-bedroom flat.

She tried patiently to make him leave. She explained that within her culture and religion, unmarried couples don't live together. She made it clear that living in Austria had not changed her. And she would not tolerate the European way of life inside her home. But nothing she said made any difference.

He was still living with them in November when her son Roy turned ten years old. Christmas and then the New Year celebration of 1981 came and went. On the seventh of January her Moosh turned thirteen.

Even if he were an angel dressed in a suit, even if he were to cover their flat with gold and diamond carpets, nothing in the world could make her accept having a live-in male friend, now that she had a teenage girl at home.

But her polite attempts failed, one after another. Being a modern European, a true Englishman through and through, he simply could not understand. And she had avoided the use of force; it could have ugly consequences for her in the office where she was still an outsider. Yet she was certain she would resort to any means if he was still there by summer when the children would be at home the whole time.

One month later, in February, she received a letter from her mother. She expected it to be a late birthday wish for Moosh. But it wasn't. Her mother stated what she was well aware of already and accused her of what she wasn't. She had sent a clear order. The letter read:

You have a young teenage girl at home, and a boy of ten years. You are neglecting your children and searching for your own personal happiness. Don't you realize what consequences it might have on them?

Within a few seconds the letter was drenched by her tears. Her mother had called her irresponsible and cheap, for having a male friend. And for allowing him to visit her at home.

You are giving them the wrong picture of what a mother should be. A wrong lesson in dignity. So if you want to stay with this man you'd better marry him. Besides, Teheran is not a safe place to live now if you are thinking of coming back. There are bombs exploding everywhere. Since Khomeini, the Islamic leader came to Teheran, all the statues of the Shah have been demolished. Everything, which had to do with 2000 years of the Persian monarchy is being destroyed. Memorial buildings, public squares, parks, all are ravaged. Tehran is ruined.

Some say there is a problem with Iraq. At the moment all we know is that it's only a border conflict. But it is not at all foreseeable what will happen next.

As she came to this part, the letter started to vanish behind the wall of her tears. All she could see was blue color spilled onto white something, which was about to disintegrate into nothing. *Mom still does not trust I could do anything right!*

That evening she was taken to urgent-care by paramedics. John and the children accompanied her. Half of her body had gone numb.

The doctors suspected a stroke, so she was told that it was crucial that she stay overnight for tests and observation. "No way," she said. "I am not staying here, I have two young children, and no one to take care of them."

But the physician insisted, "I can't let you go home. If I do, and something happens to you later, it would be a big responsibility for me."

The physician then asked her if she had somebody waiting outside. She told him that her children were there and a friend. The physician walked out the door, and a few minutes later came back with all three of them. Moosh and Roy were crying. John, who was in a state of panic himself, begged her to stay and promised to take care of her children.

While she was in the hospital, a stay of five days instead of one night, she had time to review her life. Her mother's letter had exploded in her like a volcano, pushing her to the end of the road. On the one hand, she had her obligations to consider, the strain of her responsibility to the kids. On the other hand, she didn't love this man. Yet he was her only means of survival if she didn't want to give up and return home.

John was considerate, kind, and loyal, but didn't seem to comprehend that she couldn't live with him without being married to him. Then she suddenly realized that there was nothing to think about. She had nowhere to go to. There *was* no other option than marriage. She had to do what she "had" to do.

During her absence, John succeeded in proving that he was indeed trustworthy. She asked the children hundreds of "unimportant" questions to satisfy herself, specific and clever questions regarding his manners at home. Her children laughed about her inquires, not understanding their relevance.

Finally, she made up her mind to draw a red line through her personal desires, and marry the Englishman despite her lack of love or affection for him. She knew he would, if she asked him to.

All the events of her past seemed to be reoccurring. Destiny was taking her back to where she had been at the age of nineteen. Only this time, it was thousands of miles away from home, and now she was marrying for her children's sake.

They say, "You only live once," and her life was bound to re-run, halfway through.

CHAPTER 13
Faith and The Unknown Land

Months later, John had neither moved out nor had he asked her to marry him. At the end of her patience, and tired of the wearisome struggle with herself, she told him that they had to get married if he intended to live with them any longer. She was ashamed of herself and felt contempt for having to tell him.

In April of 1982 they finally married. She was thirty-five then, and so was he. She knew it would be a boring life. Yet she was thankful that dear God had given her another chance to survive. What she didn't know was that she had done the impossible.

That day she told him: "You must always be careful of your behavior towards my children." She warned him that only one wrong move, a small incident, just one simple complaint from the children would be enough for her to kick him out and get him into serious trouble. John knew by then that she meant what she said.

But he remained a respectful, understanding and caring companion to all of them. And nothing came between them, ever, regarding the children.

He attained what he wished for, a warm family and a loyal wife. For that she was to him. And in return he tried his best to be a correct and faithful husband, and a great father to Moosh and Roy.

She helped him by working hard and giving him more time to study. Soon he completed his courses and became a qualified architect. And he did his part, by helping her financially and lending a hand in her day-to-day duties.

Toward the end of that year, however, everything that appeared perfect -- at least on the outside -- changed dramatically.

Around this time, mid 1982, the growth in Austria's economy slowed down. A large number of employees lost their jobs, and foreigners, including John, were among the first to go.

The shift in the economy affected foreigners in two ways. Not only did they lose their jobs, but hard times launched a hatred among the locals towards those aliens still at work. And she was one of them.

As employees disappeared one by one, she knew that very soon her time would come. Her boss, always so sympathetic, seemed intent on keeping her as long as he could. But as she was paid by the hour, the low volume of work decreased her income.

In such circumstances, sitting and waiting wouldn't feed the children. Her husband, having received his degree, was now qualified for a full-time job. But there was nothing in the job market, and Austria was no longer a friendly place for foreigners.

Their first thought was to move to England, where his prosperous parents lived. But she couldn't imagine asking them for help. They didn't appreciate the fact that their son had married a divorced woman, with two children from a *Third World Country*. Until the revolution, hardly anyone knew of Iran, other than the few Europeans who had worked there.

The other obstacle was that his parents had had a bad experience with his ex-wife. His ex was from Yugoslavia, a communist country. Many of the Yugoslavs who traveled to Graz, the first border-city on Austrian ground, tried to find ways to stay permanently. The best way for young girls was to marry an Austrian national. John's ex-wife discovered, however, that an English passport was even better than an Austrian one. So she made him marry her by faking a pregnancy. In his parents' opinion, she too, had married him for the same reason, so they were not counting on this marriage to last long.

Other than that, it was not easy to tell how England's economy would be in the near future. She had learned that a change of economy in one European country usually affects the whole of Europe.

Besides, going to England, some-how, just didn't feel right to her.

Her feelings reminded her of the last few months in Iran. How something within her was pushing her out of the country. How she gradually began to feel like a stranger there, and how everything looked unfamiliar to her toward the end.

She had the exact same premonition now. Something was driving her out of Europe.

Years later, it happened to her again, in another part of the world. Then, her feelings finally made sense. Her instinct was telling her that it was time to move on. Only destiny wouldn't take her to the right place until ten years later.

They consequently decided to seek employment outside Europe, starting with the United Kingdom's former colonies where John was allowed to work. Then Japan, Saudi Arabia, and Kuwait. They applied at the Australian embassy for immigration visas. In brief, they looked into every available opportunity around the world.

The only positive answer came from West Africa. The Enugu University in Nigeria offered her husband a lecture position. It came with a paid ticket for the whole family and accommodations. But not the shipping of personal belongings. John left in February, and she stayed back for the kids to finish the school year.

Inevitably, when the children were ready to leave, she had to sell everything. The household items were given away to friends or charity. Until nothing much was left in the small home that she had put together piece by piece for her children.

Losing almost all their possessions didn't bother her. But leaving the empty nest where her children had lived and grown for five years, was most difficult. So a week before their departure, she painted the flat and cleaned it up nice and shiny. And then she started packing the few remaining items that were of emotional value to her. The bits and pieces that she had kept to remind her of her past. Some dear chattels, the legacy of her culture, which had been demoted a hundred years since the revolution. They were all placed in boxes tenderly. She packed them carefully; all, which was very few, that connected her with the wrecked first-half of her existence. She closed the boxes, then wrote on each of them: Enugu Campus, University of Nigeria, Nigeria, West Africa. No return address.

❖❖❖PART V❖❖❖
LIFE IN WEST AFRICA

CHAPTER 14
Another Start from Scratch

In July 1983, they were in the huge aircraft flying to Nigeria to join her husband. She was exhausted, physically and emotionally. This time it had taken her too long to prepare the children for the move. Her Moosh was now fifteen, and little Roy was not so little anymore. He was almost thirteen.

She knew it would be a challenge to persuade them. The most crucial year of their life had been spent in that small town. They had lived the best part of their childhood in Austria, in the carefree and happy environment that she had provided for them. They were two young kids when they arrived; now they had transformed into teenagers. To them, it was like leaving home.

She had spent weeks talking to Moosh and Roy, reasoning and promising that they would have a better life in Nigeria. It was a risk, for *she* didn't know if that was true or not at the time, but it wasn't an absolute lie either. She didn't have the heart to hurt them, tell them how desperate the work situation was, but she was earnest in her belief that she would deal with it come what may. *Please, God, give me the strength.*

They arrived at the Lagos Airport at midday. As soon as they entered the arrivals' hall, the passengers disbursed in different directions.

They didn't know whom to follow. It was an enormous corridor full of people, all black, talking and milling around. Some were embracing each other, and others were walking to the right and left with their suitcases. It was hard to tell who was arriving and who was departing.

They walked towards a sign which said *CUSTOMS*, but it was not manned, so they looked around to find an official. There were a number of them wandering through the crowd, talking to everyone and to each other at the same time. No one was in a hurry, and they were all shouting as if everyone were deaf. It looked more like a social event than an airport.

The three of them were walking up and down the arrivals' lounge, not knowing where to go. Until they spotted John. He saw them too. He was standing by the exit door, and his face lit up when he saw them.

After hugs and kisses, he asked them if they had been through immigration.

"No. We couldn't find a window or a desk, or an officer."

"But you've already passed the immigration check-point," he said, surprised, but not concerned.

"Have we? We probably have. I don't remember!" She answered hesitantly.

"I don't honestly remember a thing since we got on the plane in Graz. My mind must have been absent again."

"All right, never mind, let's go to the domestic flight terminal."

This terminal was less crowded, but also nearly empty of anything. A big hall with a few windows, no stands, no officers, no information board, nothing other than numerous rows of chairs. Four wide sliding glass doors opened to the landing area. It was hot and humid, and the passengers, all local, were sitting and waiting for the aircraft to arrive. Most of them were snoozing.

They had half an hour until the next flight to Enugu, the town where the university was located, and they were going to live. So, they too, sat down.

Nearly two hours later they were still waiting. The only thing they could hear was a noisy thunderstorm and heavy rain outside. No sign of a plane, or any announcements, or computerized flight schedules. Not even a board on the wall or a hand-written one. None of the other passengers seemed worried. Nobody was going around asking what was happening, other than John who couldn't find an official anyway.

After three long hours they finally heard a voice on the loud speaker: "Passengers flying to Enugu can now board." No sooner did the speaker say the name 'Enugu' than the crowd jumped up and ran toward the doors, slid them open and charged forward.

"Well, what's the hurry?" she said. "It's pouring, and we don't have umbrellas. We'd better wait until everyone is gone, then we'll run too, so we don't get wet." She assumed that the others were running for the same reason. When the crowd was gone, they finally followed. But as they saw the plane three hundred yards away from the glass doors, they couldn't stop laughing.

Under buckets of water pouring from the sky, the passengers had gathered around the staircase. They were hastily climbing over each other, trying to get on the stairway, which was still chained. Two robust looking, black police officers were standing by the steps, pushing them away, using all their strength to get them in a line.

"I won't open the chain unless you stand in a proper line," one of the officers shouted. No one paid any attention.

She was standing a couple of yards away from the pack, laughing at this unbelievable scene, holding the children close to her side. John was one step ahead on them facing the scene with his hands stretched out to protect them. They were soaked by the rain, like four little ducks lost in the river, yet laughing as they waited for their turn to board.

They were facing a new and completely different kind of life, but somehow it didn't feel frightening. It was more amazing than scary, like watching a field full of nutty school children fighting over a new toy.

After more than half an hour, the passengers managed to rush up the stairs, three or four at the same time. When the four of them ultimately made their way into the airplane, they discovered the real reason for all the frenzy. It was not the rain. After her husband found a row of three seats together, he was still standing in the aisle.

"Why are you not sitting down somewhere?" she asked him.

"I can't find a seat. They're all taken."

"How come?" she wondered.

"The seats aren't numbered. And it looks like there are more passengers than seats. I think they sold more tickets than they have space for, but it's okay, I'll just stand by you until we land."

She couldn't stop laughing as the plane started moving before her husband completed his sentence. A smiling stewardess came to his rescue, giving him her own seat just as the plane was taking off.

Anyone who is in his fifties today might still remember the dreadful tales of the Biafran war, which dragged on for years. The name comes from the Bight of Biafra, the bay that lies on the West Coast of Africa. The battlefields were the eastern and western states of Nigeria.

Enugu is the capital of the eastern states, which was home to the Ibos. At the time of the Biafran war, they were fighting for independence. It took years for the Nigerian government to defeat them. Following a lengthy war, when it seemed beyond it's power to succeed, the government boycotted those states. Yet the Ibos didn't surrender. After a long period of resistance, they died a slow brutal death from hunger; an unfair downfall by any definition.

The mass grave of those who sacrificed their lives in vain for independence, is now the city of Enugu.

Enugu consists of three sectors. The modern sector, where the white expatriates live, the green area. The jungles are untouched except for their borders that is cultivated, and there are modern and luxurious villas complete with swimming pools and tennis courts. The residents are the employees of private, rich companies, mostly European and English.

The semi-modern section is where the educated natives such as physicians, scientists, and architects live. This is the dry land, on which the residential and business buildings are built, and has "downtown" characteristics.

And then there is the rest of the city, which houses the traditional natives, young and old. The older generations of pension age live with their children and grandchildren in large extended families. The children take care of the older generation, and grandparents look after the youngest. They don't die lonely and forgotten in a home or in their apartments, like in Europe and U.S.

Enugu shares the beauty of its landscape with the rest of Africa, a dry, dead desert where the earth is covered with red sand surrounded by jungles. The enormous university campus is in the middle of the desert, with a one-story building used for lectures and administrative offices. On the vegetated part of the campus, you can see a number of bungalows in-between the tropical trees, where the foreign lecturers live. Some bring their families, some don't.

You'll find foot-long, big and fat, orange-colored lizards that do "push-ups" while sunbathing -- which means most of the day. And the monitor lizards, even larger, which "make a good lunch," according to the natives.

When the Harmattan -- the hot, dry desert wind -- blows, it fills the air, and covers the earth and anything on it, with red layers of sand that remain for weeks. There are only two seasons in a year, six months each. The dry season which is extremely hot, and the rainy season, hot and humid.

A large part of its population consists of Moslems. They live under true Moslem rules in a united brotherhood community with others -- Christians and various native religions. Modern technology has not taken over the life of the Nigerians. The women are not veiled. They are warm, kind, and respectful toward each other, and toward the white minority. Even when the latter behave with arrogance. Many of the whites work there and receive large salaries in exchange for working in a third world country, and use the best of the country's resources, then treat the natives like underlings.

Following a mix-up in paper work, her husband didn't get a bungalow on the campus to which he was entitled. Instead they were given a second floor flat in the city, the semi-modern sector, in a large apartment complex. The building was rented by the University of Enugu for staff and lecturers.

It took her ten days to come to terms with the new home and get a feel for where they were. The flat was spacious, with three bedrooms semi-furnished. The large sitting-dining room had a balcony that overlooked the neighbor's two-story house, a middle class Ibo family. The master bedroom's window faced a large expanse of deserted land between their building and the next house. Through this window she could see across the open area, to where the native families lived.

The reason I call it an "area" is because it did not resemble a place to live. It was only a large piece of soil, red sand, with four small wooden sheds on the right, and a very small shed, the bathroom, on the left side.

That was her first exposure to the way of life of the less fortunate Ibos, as she sat by the window and watched them for hours. During this time she learned more about the reality of life and the diversity in human nature. In that place outside her bedroom window lived four or five families together, perhaps more, she couldn't tell. There were around ten adults and ten to fifteen children. The sheds were mostly used at night, and daily life took place in the open area.

It was a puzzle to her that so many people could live peacefully in one small, shared area. They had only one source of water, and that was the pipe in the middle of the land. They washed themselves and their children, who ran naked up to a certain age, with soap and water, three or four times a day.

The women washed their clothing and sheets at the same water pipe, while they talked, laughed and sang traditional songs. In early evenings, they gathered around the fire and cooked, and soon after the sun went down, they disappeared into the sheds. They had no electricity. And yet, what one could see and hear from that side was loud laughter, singing, dancing, and children happily playing. Never an angry voice, among either the adults or the children.

These observations gave her courage a boost every time she watched. After a while, she was so proud to be a part of that *unity*, that she settled for living there permanently. But destiny had a different plan in store for her. And what made them leave that beautiful, peaceful town was not their decision.

CHAPTER 15
The Country of Many Friends

A few days after she recovered from the trauma of the big move, she went to work turning the flat into a home for the children. She unpacked the art works from Esfahan, ornaments and souvenirs, the family pictures, and the crochet pieces made by her mother's own hand. She decorated the place like a traditional Persian home.

In less than a month the children were registered in the best local school, called the government school of Nigeria. There were special schools for the white expatriates, but she wanted Moosh and Roy to go to a local school. The education system was the same both ways -- the English system. But she hoped for her children to learn from the gracious, selfless, and respectful nature of the Nigerians. So they would notice what difference it makes being that way in the life of those around one.

The children weren't opposed, but they felt strange, going to a school where they were the only two white students. When she told them her reasons for sending them to a local school, they became curious and gave her the benefit of the doubt.

Years later when both Moosh and Roy matured into cheerful, benevolent and easy-going grownups, she knew that she had been right.

The only problem they had at the time was that the official

language at schools in Enugu was English. And at their school they had to learn Ibo, the native language, as a second language. They did have a little knowledge of English, but not enough to enhance their studies. Now that they were older, mastering a third language, was a concern to them.

She encouraged them continuously: "Look, the English language is much easier than German. You went to school in Austria with zero knowledge and see how beautifully you managed. Now you even know some English, so for you, this is nothing compared with five years ago. You did it then, you are going to do it again." And she promised them: "Go on and try your best. If you find that you can't do it, we'll move away at the end of the year."

They were satisfied. Maybe they thought they had to show Mom, that she was not always right, which was okay with her. That gave them courage. They looked at it as an adventure.

They never knew how desperate their mother was. They just relied on the fact that she would do anything to help, should they run into trouble. And they were right. No matter how and where, she would have taken them out of the country if they were going to have serious problems at school. But somehow, she was confident that if they were going to have difficulties, it wouldn't be because of the language or the people.

John who had taken the week off, went back to work the next Monday. She and the children began investigating the area to find out where and how they could get what they needed. The children, having their own bedrooms now, were excited and had various ideas on how to decorate them. They also needed to buy accessories for the kitchen, bathroom, and bedrooms.

She had some savings left and although it was not enough for a car (which was an absolute necessity in Enugu), she could afford to decorate. The walls were bright green, which none of them liked, and they were not allowed to paint, so the children brightened them with pictures and posters. The floors were linoleum, and didn't require Rugs because of the hot weather, they were told.

So they composed a long shopping list and went out in search of stores. That Monday was the first time they were going out of the house without John, in a part of the city where no white people lived.

The building's entrance opened to the side road. From there, they turned left and a few yards further they reached a T junction. On their left, the street made a sharp bend and they couldn't see much, so they didn't dare to go that way. They chose the right, that led up a steep hill, and walked on.

Every few yards, on the shady side of the road, there were small wooden stands; the street looked like a little Sunday market place, each one had a sign on top that said: *Supermarket!*

A lot of women were around, some sold fruits and vegetables, others buying them. There were few men, but a large number of children. Yet no one was hanging around idly; each one was doing something, or going somewhere. They all seemed to have a purpose for being there.

Later, after the family had lived in Enugu for a few months, they learned why there were more women around than men. In Africa, women are truly equal to men, they have what others are still fighting for, all over the world. They take part in heavy labor such as mixing concrete at building sites and carrying it in large pans on their head. And there is no question about their dominant role in family life. This is the reason of this strong bond among family members and the community. Their ties are stronger than anywhere else in the world, for they have a foundation of unity, like nowhere else.

Around noon time, the smell of cooked yams and boiled rice filled the air; unfamiliar, but not unpleasant, mixed with the smell of hot sand, scattered around with every footstep.

As the three of them were passing the stands, the women gave them a smile and a hand wave. The children only said: "Onioja" -- it meant foreigner -- in a friendly tone of voice, accompanied by a surprised look in their eyes which took only a few seconds and then they passed. It was like calling "Hi, you."

Some women were carrying loads of yams, fruits or vegetables in a basket on their head, and would only hold it when they turned around. Their burdens looked heavy, but they were smiling and talking to each other as if they were wearing nothing heavier than a pretty hat. The women were clean and happy, so were the children. Plus, they were little beauties, especially their eyes. Some had such beautiful eyes that it was hard to look into them for more than a moment.

That day they walked up to the main road and discovered that from there they could get a taxi or bus to anywhere they wanted to go. But they decided not to travel much further; they would just buy some fruit and return. It was getting too hot. They realized that for a long shopping day, they had to start very early like everyone else. Besides, the fear of the unknown somehow held them back.

Their first day went smoothly. They'd received a much warmer reception, than they had experienced in Europe -- more human, more friendly. And most surprising of all, even though they were the only whites in the neighborhood, they were not made to feel outsiders.

Time passed. When they had arrived in Nigeria, the rainy season was ending. Now, it was getting hotter by the hour. Their flat wasn't air-conditioned although it was in one of the new and modern buildings. And there were no telephone lines. They did have a refrigerator with a freezer, but they needed to buy fans for every room, and a special filter for drinking water. They were warned that the water had to be boiled first, and then poured into the container. After it filtered to the bottom, which took days, it was drinkable. By the time they finally got everything they needed, she had no savings left.

Before September, when the children were to start school, they had experienced two extremely hot months and more difficulties. They faced the first one when they went to the post office to call Teheran, and advise the family of their safe arrival. Since the revolution she had received two letters from Iran, and both had been opened. When they realized that the mail was being censored, they decided to communicate by phone.

That early morning they took a taxi to the post office. They were expecting an office with a counter and a staff, but there was just a big room with a small empty desk on one side, and three telephone kiosks on the opposite wall, and that was it.

The person sitting behind the desk had his head on his folded arms resting on the desk. They went nearer, to the middle of the room and said, "Halloo." He didn't answer. "Excuse me." No response. So they ventured closer and saw that the man's eyes were shut.

She repeated her greeting her voice just a bit louder: "Sorry, sir, we would like to make a long distance call." The clerk raised his head "There are no lines today. Come back tomorrow," then he put his head down and closed his eyes again. He had been asleep the whole time.

They looked at each other, stunned.

"I think we woke him up," Moosh said embarrassed. "He's angry with us. Let's go home."

At home, they told John the story, he just laughed. He explained: "Don't worry. Go back tomorrow. This is how things work here. The poor man at the post office probably doesn't know if and when they'll have a connection to the rest of the world." Now she understood why the day they arrived at the airport and she told John that there was no one at the customs desk he was not surprised or worried too much.

They tried again the next day. "Oh, sorry, Madam, the lines were cut off just five minutes ago. Come back tomorrow." Tomorrow didn't come until ten days later, when they finally managed to get through to Teheran.

Soon they learned. They couldn't go to the post office to make a call as they needed, but just anytime and often. As John made clear, "in Enugu everything works like that." Nobody is in a hurry for anything. And no customer gets angry. If a task couldn't be done today, there was always a tomorrow and the day after, and the time in-between, the people in charge would take a nap.

They soon discovered the reasons behind the "maniana" philosophy. It was the extreme heat, humidity, and a helplessly corrupt government.

Life was not easy for them in Enugu, but is it anywhere, for anyone? It just depends how strong we are in dealing with it. The most important source of strength, in my view, is having a purpose and believing in it. And next, is having a point of refuge during times of despair, where we can recover, and regain the strength we need to move on. It can be anything; religion, an object, a person, a place, or the creation itself. As long as we believe, anything works.

A month later, it was such unbearable heat that they had to douse themselves with water a few times a day, and wear a minimum of clothing to make it through the day, the electricity went off. No fan, no refrigerator, and after three days the freezer started to melt. It was not just their flat, the whole area had gone dark. When the sun went down, the night was pitch black, and they couldn't see anything, not even the people standing near them.

The first night was freaky. They had heard stories of armed robberies, and people who were killed by burglars. For that reason every building in the semi-modern area had a night watchman on duty. But in that darkness a black person in a gray uniform was hard to spot, so the watchmen found themselves a comfortable place and took a nap as soon as they could.

One night they heard shots and screams coming from the house opposite the sitting room. It went on for an hour, with cries for help and people running and things falling. Then they heard a car driving away, and then silence.

A few minutes later a neighbor knocked on their door. He was a young Nigerian physician with whom they had become friends. He lived with his family in the opposite flat. When they opened the door and recognized him in the candle light, they let him in. He had come to comfort them.

"Did you hear it?" He asked.

"Yes, what was going on?"

"An armed robbery, but they got away. The police are looking for them in the area. You'd better lock your doors and close the windows. The thieves are on the run and might be looking for a place to hide."

They thanked him. John offered the doctor a warm beer and asked him to stay for a while. He didn't intend to leave quickly, he assured them. That night he stayed for hours to see them through this odd experience. He was a cheerful, jolly, and talkative person. He talked the whole time, telling them the story of his life and all about his large family. Then he went on with funny jokes, and by the time he left, he had cheered them up considerably.

Locking the door was one thing, but closing the windows was unthinkable. They opened the windows as soon as he left. Moosh had developed asthma when she had turned thirteen, and she couldn't breathe in that standing, hot and humid air.

The moral support they got from the understanding and caring neighbor and others they soon met, made it easier for them to deal with the hardships. At the end of the week the electricity returned. By this time the food in the refrigerator and freezer had to be thrown out. But they didn't die of hunger or heat.

She took her family through the physical and psychological strain of those difficult periods by being strong herself. The children watched her reactions carefully to estimate the seriousness of the situation. By making the whole experience seem like an adventure, little by little, she could feel that her children were becoming stronger and tougher.

A couple of weeks later, they were without tap water. They asked their opposite neighbor, the doctor, what they should do. "There is a well nearby. I usually send the boy who works for us to bring us some. Give him any container you have. He can go a few times more and bring some for you," the friendly neighbor suggested.

The water shut-off lasted ten days. Every day the little boy would go often to the well and back, which was miles away, and bring water for both families. Just enough for drinking and cooking. They washed using as little as possible, taking clues as they watched the natives from the bedroom window.

Those poor people had just a few pots and pans, so everyone would take a bowl, and they'd go to the well in groups, countless times a day. When they returned, the first thing they did was wash their bodies with the water of a medium size bowl, the way only they knew how! And so they were always clean.

She used to take the minibus from the main road every second day to go grocery shopping at the bazaar, for it was cheaper than the "supermarkets" nearby. It was a half-hour drive, and the minibus held twelve passengers mostly locals. They often carried chicken, or goats, or some animal with them that they had bought, or were taking to the bazaar for sale. But despite the sweltering heat, they never smelled, nor did the minibus, as unbelievable as it might sound. Years later when she was traveling in London's underground, it was a different story; in a country where people think of themselves as modern, civilized, and more intelligent than any race in the world.

Two weeks before school began they made an excursion to visit the school ground. Also to find out how they should get there, and how long it would take. The school was a large two-story building in the middle of the desert, built on a little slope of earth. There was a three-foot high fence around it, and a security officer was sitting in a small wooden shed outside the fence to the left of the gate, snoozing. They arrived by taxi, and asked him if they could get inside to have a look. "No problem," he said.

It was a twenty minute walk to the building. The walkway was leveled but not asphalted. The classrooms were built in rows on four sides of a square inner yard on two levels. There was a narrow opening to the right side of the building connecting the inner yard with outside. Each classroom on the first floor had two doors, one opening to the inner yard and one to the outside of the building.

The second floor was exactly the same, but the outside doors opened onto a balcony that circled the building in one piece, shared by all the classrooms.

Although it was quiet that day, the whole atmosphere spoke of children, life, modesty, and hope. The scent of chalk in the air was combined with the reassuring odor of hot sand rising in the intense heat.

Those who suffer from a fear of heights would understand the comforting feeling of being well-grounded. In West Africa, especially through the dry season, that distinct odor of the heat and hot sand is always in the air. It attaches one to the earth and radiates a feeling of oneness, of being connected to the earth and to each other.

Maybe that's why there is a stronger bond between these people, to the earth and the air. I think this is one of the reasons why people there live together with such unity, where the sense of "one for all and all for one," still exists. It hasn't died like in the coldness of Europe.

On the fifth of September the children were ready for school. They were required to wear uniforms, white shirts and navy skirts for the girls, and white shirts and navy shorts for the boys. But Moosh and Roy didn't complain. They acted like heroes, looking forward to yet another adventure. John took them to school in a taxi, and would pick them up in the afternoon.

That afternoon she was waiting for them, anxious to hear about their first impressions. They arrived excited, loud and lively.

"You know, Mom, we are the only whites in the whole school." They said almost simultaneously.

"Did you have any problems?"

"No, the only problem is that they speak English in a very strange accent. It's too hard to understand."

She reassured them that it wouldn't take long before they would get used to it and understand much better. "Were they friendly to you?" she asked.

"Oh, yes, they are very nice, Mom, they helped us find our classroom, our place. They were even fighting over us, because everybody wanted to sit next to us."

She was relieved to hear that. Now, everything was settling in, and their routine life could begin.

While everyone was gone, she attended to the house. Cooking, cleaning and making it more homey. Moosh needed curtains for the windows of her bedroom. She used a beautiful hand-made bed-cover from Esfahan, where she was born. It was packed in one of the boxes among the other souvenirs. She took it out and made it into a beautiful curtain for Moosh's room.

She was content and peaceful in the home she had made. Life in Africa was laborious, but not painful. The physical strain didn't affect her as much as the psychological pressure she had been confronted with in Europe.

Her heart never ached again as it did day by day during her few months in Austria while she still worked during the recession. Her Austrian co-workers all came to the office carrying a badge pinned on their chest that said: "Go home foreigner." *How cruel people can become when they have to share,* she always thought, noticeably embarrassed, even though ignoring them.

Three weeks later she became an active member of Enugu society, once again through her children. One day Moosh came home from school and said: "Mom, one of my school mates needs some help in math. I told her you always help me, so can she come here after school so you can work with her too? Would you do it for her?"

"Of course I would."

The next day Moosh came in with her school mate. She helped them both with their math homework. The little friend was so eager to learn and extremely intelligent. The day after, when she was leaving the house she asked if her sister might come with her tomorrow. And then still another friend.

In a short period of time, over fifteen girls and boys began coming to their house to get help with their homework. In a month's time the group grew so large that she had to divide them into different hours so she could attend to them all.

Working with the children always made her happy. They loved her and she loved them. It turned into an exhausting job, but she thrived on it and enjoyed it. The reward was fulfillment. She was thrilled that they came, just because they wanted to learn. No one sent them. And she never asked for money. There was no force behind those little creatures to come to her house each day, in groups of five or six, to learn English and math.

When the wife of the friendly opposite neighbor, the doctor, gave birth to a baby girl, she instructed her about hygiene and nutrition. As well as how to raise the baby, how to teach and discipline her.

Soon, everyone in the neighborhood began flocking to her door. Her whole family had become a member of that united black community. And she was more than happy to stay there for good.

If someone had told her that she would be in England the next year, at the same time, she would have taken it as a joke. But it happened.

Following a series of strange events, they soon had to leave their dream home forever.

CHAPTER 16
The Revolutionary Nigerians

It was around 7 p.m., and they were getting ready to leave. In that part of Nigeria, Christmas time was quiet. On New Year's Eve 1984, one of the whites in the modern section of town had invited them to a party.

The radio was on, as usual, and suddenly they heard a news flash: *"There has been a military takeover in Nigeria. Government officials have been arrested. From today on there will be a 10 p.m. curfew in force. No one should be seen on the roads after ten, or they will be executed."*

It was shocking news. The family sat by the radio huddled together to hear of what came next. After half an hour the doorbell rang. It was a white colleague of John's, the only white who had ever entered their house. He was going to give them a ride to the party. He didn't seem bothered by the events. "Don't worry, let's go, we'll come back before ten. We've seen a lot of these, they usually leave us -- the English -- out of it," he assured them. And they left.

The party was one of those distinctly posh colonial gatherings. Something that she had only seen in the movies. A crowded garden party with about a hundred and fifty guests. Every important white member of the embassies were there, including the British cultural attaché who later told them that he had been in Teheran until the revolution and had beautiful memories of Iran. He even spoke a little Farsi.

After the first round of drinks, the British attaché approached

John. He was a middle-aged gentleman, humble, friendly, and well-mannered. Soon they became engaged in a long, friendly talk. She was standing by the dinner table with the children and was watching them out of the corner of her eye. She was thinking: *This is a true, well educated English-man. They must **all** be like that in England; the height of manners, the real gentlemen.*

Half an hour later John came over. "Did you ask him about the coup d'etat?" She asked, growing more worried by the minute. "Nobody seems to have any intention of leaving early."

"No," her husband answered. "The attaché says we don't need to be concerned. Even if they stopped us on the way back, they wouldn't do anything to us. But he did advise me to send your passports to the embassy and apply for permanent residency for England. He said because we're married you'll get it quickly. It's wise to do it quickly, so we can go there, should it come to an emergency evacuation."

John then added, "Look, these people have lived here for years, some of them, most of their lives. If they aren't taking the curfew seriously, why should we? Maybe they know something we don't." At this moment he spotted some university professors, and moved on to chat with them.

She stood there with the children, watching the show. In her eyes the posh party *was* just a charade. Women were showing off their dresses, their jewelry, while the few "important" blacks were left out. Others were standing in groups pretending to talk with one another, but their eyes were in constant motion. None of them seemed to be listening, because their lips were doing all the work.

At 9:30p.m. most of them were so drunk they didn't know where they were, or whom they were talking to. Some distorted creatures were rolling over each other with the music, which made the place look like a garden full of rain worms.

At this point she merely wanted to go home. "Moosh, take Roy's hand, we'll look for Dad." And so they did. After a fifteen minute search they still had not found him. They asked some guests who knew him from university. That was when she realized that they were so drunk, they barely knew their own names.

Finally a waitress found her husband unconscious on the bathroom floor, soiled and wet with his vomit. When they saw him that way, the children were stunned. She felt so humiliated. "Can you get a waiter to help us carry him out?" she asked them desperately.

With the help of two waiters, they took him outside, put him in a taxi, and headed home. It was well past ten o'clock, and the roads were totally empty, but nothing happened out of the ordinary.

The next day she got into a hefty argument with her husband. It was not their first, but certainly the worst. She was only grateful that he never got physical when they argued.

In the end, when he realized how embarrassed she'd been finding him in that state, he promised never to drink again. And he has kept his promise, all these years.

The next day, while her husband was at work, she took the children out to see what was going on. They didn't see anything abnormal on the side roads. People were around and life was going on as usual. But, there was busy traffic on the main road, gray jeeps filled with black soldiers in battle uniform, with big gray shotguns. There were also a number of soldiers walking up and down the main roads, as if watching the civilians.

Fortunately the children were out of school for a week, so they had time to wait and see what was coming next. When the day came for them to go back to school, everything seemed normal enough, and nothing happened at school according to the children when they returned.

But gradually things changed. One week later when she went to the bazaar for grocery shopping, there was hardly anything to buy. It got worse day by day until the new government rationed food items. And then rationing was extended to other commodities.

Every day she had to stand in line for hours under the burning sun along with the natives to do shopping. She was the only white person among them.

Each food item was sold separately. That meant that there was a long line for rice, another for cooking oil, and still another one for detergent and soap. Fruit and vegetables were sold somewhere else.

Sometimes she had to stand in line half the day only to be told: "Sorry, no more meat. Sorry, no more butter. Sorry, no more soap." And those shop owners who did have those goods -- black market -- asked for any price they wanted.

Prices were going up by the day and the bazaar was becoming emptier. The soldiers were everywhere now, to maintain the peace, as fights frequently broke out at every place selling groceries or household goods.

She didn't mind the fights, as they were not violent, they were only hungry. But as a consequence of the high prices, their budget got tighter and tighter. Until one day the worst of her fears became reality.

The new government announced that the paper money was going to change face. By the announced deadline everyone had to bring their bills to the bank and exchange with the new bills. After the deadline, the old Niara bills (Nigerian currency) would be worthless.

Considering the fact that the banking craze of using checks or credit cards were not adopted in Nigeria, this was a disaster.

The Nigerians, even most of the businessmen, didn't keep their money in banks. This could be one reason why the economy has failed to flourish.

Now, with the country's new legal tender, thousands of people who had hidden their life savings in the pillow-covers or under the ground, had to dig them out, take them to the bank and receive the new money. The result was absolute chaos.

Each time she or her husband attempted to go to the bank, the only one in that part of the town, the area looked like a war zone. People were waiting in front of the building from the early morning hours, long before it opened. And when the doors were finally unlocked, they attacked. Hundreds of them. And the soldiers couldn't do much to keep order, other than beating them with batons or heavy chains to hold them back.

Then within the first few hours, the bank would run out of new bills and send away the hundreds who were still fighting to get in.

Life was getting harder for them and for the Ibos. But there was a distinct variation between the kind of difficulties faced by Nigerians, and those of civilized countries. From her experiences living in Europe, and Iran, the Ibos's troubles were not the result of modernization, improved technology, or just old-fashioned greed.

In spite of all the turmoil, life was not that tough for the whites living in the modern section of the town in Enugu. They didn't have to go through any of the hassle. They had a black cook; another did their shopping and ran their errands. They had their private generators for electricity shut offs, and a spare water tank for water emergencies. So they couldn't grasp what the natives had to deal with. And when they passed a bank or a food line, and saw the desperate efforts of the public to supply their basic needs, they would call it "the wild behavior of the uneducated." The "mis-conception" was just the effect of the attitude of non-natives.

John and she however, enjoyed living in that sector, and even when John told her that they finally were assigned a bungalow on the university campus, she refused to move.

She argued: "I have lived in Europe, in Iran, as it was one of the most modern countries in the world, although the rest of the world was unaware. Believe me, the first time I set foot in Europe, I was disappointed. We had learned so much about modern Europe at school, but from what I saw, they were decades behind the Iran that I knew."

"And even though they act as the best of the human race, I have encountered the inhumane, depressed and rough nature of most of them. So, now that I have the choice, I prefer living in this area. I feel I belong to this neighborhood. I love being surrounded by these true-hearted folk. To say the least, I am welcome here. They need me and I need them, and I wish to stay around."

Meanwhile the news from Teheran was not any better than in Nigeria. The border conflict with Iraq that had started in 1980 had expanded into the capital city, and become a blood-thirsty war, now going on four years.

She could no longer call home so easily, so she tried to write. According to the letters she received from Teheran, the family was growing despite revolution and war. Her younger sister who had a baby girl when they left, had given birth to a second child, a boy. Her brother, who had been married almost for seven years, had now his first child, a little girl. But the news was horrifying:

The bombs are falling from the sky like hail. We are living in the basement most of the time. The country is destroyed by revolutionaries. Food is rationed but no one dares go out and stand in line. You never know when the Iraqis will attack.

There have been so many casualties. It's impossible to keep count. There are rumors that masses of people, young and old, are being sent to stand in front of the Iraqis' tanks -- in the name of Islam. Young children are being sent to walk on the minefields to clear the area for the soldiers.

A rumor is going around that every morning a truck stops by the schools, full of children. A soldier goes in. He carries a lot of keys with him and guns. He walks into the classrooms and speaks for the children: "We are fighting against the infidels. Anybody who wants to go to heaven can join me. We go to the front. I'll give you a gun, and one of these keys. These are the keys to heaven. If you survive, you'll have defended Islam. If you die, you'll be a martyr for Islam and go straight to heaven for you're holding the key to eternal life."

Apparently many children join in these suicide missions. They are told they don't need to ask their parents' permission, for they are doing this for God. Then they are taken straight-away to the front in that truck.

In March, nine months after their arrival in Enugu, she received a letter from her sister, Shana. That letter was the basis of the next big change in their lives. She wrote:

My older son is soon fourteen now. So I don't know how long I can keep him here. Six years have passed since the revolution. You can imagine, a child who was ten years old at the time, is now a young man of sixteen. During this time they have learned that they must fight in the name of Allah. The kids have grown up with the idea. They don't know anything else. So I have decided to leave the country. Austria is at the moment the only European country that will give us a tourist visa. So I am going to leave by the end of this school year. If your bank account in Austria is still open, let me know. We are planning to sell the house and car and send the money into your account through the black market money-handlers. I want to start now, so I'll be ready by summer when they finish school.

My husband can't come with us this summer; he'll join us later. Please answer as quickly as you can.

Shana

She answered her sister's letter the same day, giving her the account number and address. But she was terribly concerned. She could imagine how difficult it would be for Shana, especially since she didn't speak German. Yet the news from Iran was disturbing; she was right to get out and rescue her sons.

The news about life in Iran destroyed her last hope of ever going back. And it reinforced her decision to stay in West Africa forever. She was happy there, and the children were coping well. Moosh and Roy had made a huge number of friends in the neighborhood and at school. One of Moosh's school mates had offered them a ride to school and back every day. They had been totally accepted by the teachers and their peers. The fact that they were the only whites at school had never become an issue. And by now, they didn't feel they were any different from the others.

She was pleased to see that they were growing up to be so open-minded. The black children had generously included them from day one. And this helped them understand how important it was to not judge people by their appearance or race.

The long shopping days and endless lines went on, the soldiers with their heavy shotguns looked more fierce than they acted. She was able to move around without fear or restriction. On nights without electricity, she worked with the children by candlelight in the unbearable heat. And on days with no water, everyone volunteered to fetch it for them, and they saved it in big containers that she had stocked for that purpose. All in all, she guarded their happiness steadfastly from being taken away by the difficulties of life there.

When the deadline for changing money arrived, they had not yet managed to get any. Every time they tried, there was panic in front of the bank, chaos and fights. Then the bank closed before they could get in.

The Ibos were going through a rough time, and it was heartbreaking to witness their struggle to survive. And she counted herself as one of them. The last day she tried one more time, but it was hopeless.

They needed food, and she didn't have any money to shop that day. So using some small change, she took a taxi and went to the bazaar. When she arrived at the stand where she was accustomed to shop, she asked the jolly shop owner if he would make an exception, and take her old bills, as she hadn't been able to change them. "No, ma'm. I can't take 'm." It wasn't surprising. The bank had closed for the day and the deadline had passed. Time had run out and now no shop owner would accept the defunct currency.

She knew he had no choice, so she didn't insist. She stood there not knowing what to do next. Looking desperate, she asked herself, *does this mean we'll starve until John gets new bills at the end of the month? What other way is there to shop for food?* She was thinking.

A male voice interrupted her thoughts. "Look, ma'm, take whatever you need for a week or more, and then pay when you have the new money. It's only two more weeks to the end of the month." It was the friendly shop owner coming to her rescue.

She couldn't believe her ears. The man didn't even know her name. She lived in the north of the city, and the bazaar was in the south. But here he was, in the same trouble himself, and maybe even worse, giving her food, and allowing her to pay later. To her, his generosity was most unbelievable and in the last place on the earth that someone might expect. This stranger had trusted her on the basis of nothing. She took his offer, thanked him, and gratefully paid him off, and a little more at the end of the month.

The water problem solved itself by the end of the dry season. The first day it rained after six months, they'd gone two weeks without tap water.

That day began with the voice of a child on the street singing: "It's raining, it's raining!" She looked out the window, but saw nothing. Just a few minutes later it was pouring down, like nothing she had ever seen before. The sky and the earth seemed to be connected by a sheet of water.

On the street there was a folk-fest. After six months of such heat and the hot red sand swirling in the air with every gust of wind, this was a true blessing. It had been so hot that even the sand didn't sit for long after the wind swept across the desert. Women, young and old, and children ran outside. They were dancing, singing and washing themselves in the beautiful silver rain. She did too, joining her neighbors in celebration.

In April of that year they sent their passports to the English embassy for their visas, as they'd been advised by the British attaché. They came back within two weeks with their permanent visas for the UK.

Shortly after, she received another letter from her sister Shana, saying that they would be leaving Teheran by the end of May.

It was both good and bad news. She was happy for her sister getting out of that hell, but she wasn't sure how Shana was going to manage. Especially since the Persian friend who had helped her at the time was now in Iran. She couldn't keep calm not knowing what would happen to her sister. She had not forgotten the shock of her first day in Austria. This was the first time that Shana would be traveling without her husband, and she'd be facing a strange new world all alone.

For a time she dreamed of going to Austria to help Shana get through the first few weeks. But her savings were used up and their budget didn't allow such luxury, even though her husband agreed to stay behind. Yet she didn't intend to dream for long. So one day she took some of her jewelry and headed to the bazaar. The money she received was enough for the trip.

She planned on leaving with the children, one week before her sister was to arrive. They got their Austrian visas and bought return tickets, and waited for Moosh and Roy to finish the school year. When the day came, John flew with them to the Lagos Airport to see them off on their well-deserved vacation, as he called it. Never dreaming that instead of Austria, his family was going to end up in jail in England.

PART VI
THE FLIGHT TO ENGLAND

CHAPTER 17
The Day in Jail

They arrived at Lagos Airport and made their way to the departure area. There was the same chaos as the first day they had arrived; only now the soldiers armed with machine-guns were added to it. Big crowds swarmed through the corridors. But this time everything made sense to her. When she looked around, she could tell what everyone was doing. It was a goal-motivated chaos, which didn't seem strange at all.

A large group of passengers, all blacks, were gathering in front of the desk waiting for their boarding tickets. Nigerians used to travel to Europe frequently both for business and pleasure. The check-in desk was still empty, and the waiting passengers who were not standing in line as usual, were gathered around the desk, talking happily and laughing loudly.

So the four of them joined in and were received with friendly smiles. They chatted with them about the trip, the heat and humidity, and the story of their long wait.

Half an hour later an officer appeared behind the desk, a soldier standing by his side. The passengers attacked as they saw him and the soldiers shouted, "You have to listen to me first! We are not giving out boarding passes yet." The crowd relaxed and moved back a little.

The soldier then announced, "There is a slight problem. The direct flight to Austria has been canceled. We have arranged another flight which stops in London. From there, you'll get an immediate connection to Austria." He went on, "But for boarding cards, you must first stand in line."

The presence of the soldier made everyone obey. They stood in a proper line, handed their luggage over, and received their boarding passes in an orderly fashion.

One hour later than scheduled, the time came to say good-by and get aboard. She reminded her husband of his necessary duties in her absence and they all kissed him good-bye. "It won't be long," she assured John as she saw him wiping his wet eyes. "We'll be back in a month."

"I hope everything goes well with your sister's move. Give her my regards," he said.

The plane took off smoothly. They were all excited. She was meeting her sister after a long separation, and hoped to hear from her, in detail, about the state of affairs in Iran. Half an hour later a handsome black pilot approached Moosh and Roy, "Would you like to go with me to the cockpit, and see how the aircraft is flown?"

Thrilled, they turned to her, "Mom?"

"Sure, go on," she allowed them.

Once the children left, she relaxed in her seat and gazed out the window. The sun was shining; and beneath, there was only a thick sea of white.

Going to Austria brought back mixed memories of all she had gone through. Their nice little flat that someone else was using now. Waking up every morning to the sound of bells ringing on the roof of the church outside her bedroom. She could still hear the familiar clang of the bells; she never realized how much she had missed them. Then she thought of the people there and their problems. They seemed so insignificant compared to what the blacks were enduring in Enugu.

From her vantage point in the sky, the world below looked so unreal. She thought of the people down there on the earth rushing around, deceiving and hurting each other, some struggling just to survive, others fighting greedily to gain more. Some build, others destroy. She saw them all like little robots, racing, rushing toward the finishing-line. Then, when they finally "arrive," they fall, dog-tired and empty of spirit to find true happiness, and then they die.

She was thinking maybe that's why some say, to *the mighty God, all the beings are equal. If God is looking at us from the heavens, then everyone would look the same.*

When they reached the sky over London, she was worn out. But the children were lively and happy, trying to guess what their cousins looked like now, after all this time. They had been chatting with each other since they came back from the cockpit, so impressed and honored to have been there.

"Mom, I tell you, it's so easy, I could fly a plane, really." Roy kept repeating loudly. In fact, this did become one of his career dreams in high school.

Finally the plane touched down and they made it to the arrival hall for international flights. As they were flying to Austria on the next plane, she expected to see a flight attendant who would escort them to it. But that didn't happen. When they approached the immigration check point, she felt something was wrong. She saw an officer standing by the line of passengers, leading to the check out window, "Please, how do we get to the European flight terminal? We are going to fly to Austria from here."

The officer looked at her suspiciously, "There is no flight to Austria today, the first one is in three days."

"But we were told in Lagos that we would be flying today," she explained.

"No ma'm, I just told you, there is no flight today. It must have been a mistake. Until then, you'll have to check out and stay in a hotel, unless you know someone in London to stay with."

She didn't understand what was happening, but as they had their visa to stay in England, she settled to do what the apathetic looking officer was telling her and joined the line. But he wouldn't let go. He followed them. "Can I see your passports please."

She handed them over and murmured, "We'll have to find a hotel."

He took a careful look at their passports and then looked around, "Where is your husband?"

"He is not traveling with us. Why?"

"Because you can't enter the country without your husband." She was more puzzled now. It must be a mistake, she was thinking.

"Please come with me to the immigration office to see what we can do."

She heard the officer again; assuming he was going to help them, she thanked him, "How nice of you."

He took them in the office. There, she was told that the Lagos Airport had given them wrong information, there *was* no immediate flight to Austria. And it was confirmed that they weren't allowed to enter the United Kingdom without her husband. Not even to spend the night in a hotel.

"What do we do now?" She asked.

"We have to send you back to Nigeria," the officer answered icily, "but there is no flight to Nigeria for the next two days." He was talking as if reporting the weather 'for the next two days.'

"Can we go to my father in-law? He is a British citizen; he lives in Guildford. It is only half an hour drive from London."

The immigration officer looked at her from the top of his nose, "Do you understand English?"

"Well, I am speaking English, aren't I?" she answered impatiently.

He obviously didn't like her way of talking. "You don't understand; I repeat, you...can...not...enter...the...United Kingdom...without...your...husband," stressing every single one of his words.

Then she asked if they please could call her father in-law. "Maybe his solicitor could do something." At this point the officer went mad. Holding on to their passports, he turned around and ordered them to follow him.

He guided them through the back hallway where every door had the sign "staff only." Arms outstretched, he herded them like a herd of black sheep, up and down stairways, and into the staff elevators. Until they found themselves in the open air on the edge of the huge runway of London airport. A white airport van was waiting for them, and the officer ordered them to get in.

She was scared to death, and so were the children, but they were silent. The car had a metal screen between the back and front seat. He placed them in the back and took a seat beside the driver. "Where are you taking us?" she kept asking. They played deaf. And the driver started the car.

He drove along the runway for fifteen minutes, then stopped in front of a small building. The officer got out and told them to follow him, then led them into the building.

They entered a half-dark long and tight hallway with doors on each side. He opened the first door on his left and told them to go in and wait. The officer closed the door and left immediately with their passports, before they could say a word.

In that small room there was nothing except six chairs, chained to each other, in two facing rows, by the right and left wall.

Thank God, there are three on one side, She thought. So she took the chair in the middle, and placed Moosh and Roy on either side. "He'll be back soon, it's only a misunderstanding," she assured them, trying not to look concerned, as she put her arms around them. As time went by and the officer didn't return, she gradually held them closer; let their heads rest on her shoulders, rubbing their backs so they get a short nap.

She had no watch, so she couldn't tell how much time had passed. Jet-lag and the time difference between the two continents had her traveling in a timeless zone. The three of them dozed off, on and off, sitting on the chair.

It felt like an eternity, until another officer came in with some sandwiches. She quickly asked what time it was, and what day. "What is going to happen to us now?" He didn't answer.

Sometime later yet another officer came in and told them to follow him. He took them through the long hallway to another room. This room was also empty except for a couple of chairs. He told them to sit there and wait. She looked around. Opposite the entrance, there was another closed door. Above it was a sign that said: X-Ray.

They were called in one by one and had chest X-Rays taken. She went last. As she stood in the cubicle, she saw a calendar on the wall. It was two days since they had arrived from Africa. And the nurse told her that it was 9:30 in the morning.

What happened between that morning, and the time they were finally sitting in the departure lounge at the London airport, she still cannot remember. The unorthodox way the English bureaucracy had interrupted their trip, and their harsh treatment left a dark spot in her memory.

"We are looking for seats on the first connection to Austria. We'll get you on, if we can find any." She heard a civilian talking to her, while she was looking at the floor and thinking. At first she noticed his shiny shoes, then his designer black suit and tie.

"But we haven't gotten our passports back," she explained baffled, feeling a wave of panic.

"You will, as soon as you are inside the plane."

Her thoughts were with her sister Shana at that moment. She had promised her, in the letter from Nigeria, that she would be in Graz at least two days before they arrived from Teheran.

After hours of waiting, they were taken through the landing area to a departing aircraft. Their escort asked the stewardess if they had any passengers who had not arrived. The answer was no. So they went back all the way to the departure lounge, and made to wait for the next Austrian-bound plane. And the civilian officer disappeared.

During most of that endless day, they were shuttled back and forth to outgoing planes by different officers, in search of three vacant places.

Finally they were found. A tall, blond officer accompanied them up to their seats. He handed their passports to the flight attendant, and made sure that they'd only receive them when they were leaving the plane in Austria.

When they entered the small arrival hall of Graz Airport, she took a deep, relieved breath. There, she spotted her sister, Shana, with her two boys. As the two sisters ran to each other, she was thinking, *Thank God, we arrived just on time. What would have happened to my poor sister if that last plane in England didn't have room for us?*

If she had missed them, she'd have lost them; and all her efforts to be there for her -- from selling her jewelry to the ordeal in the customs jail in London -- would have been good-for-nothing.

She learned that Shana and the boys had just arrived from Teheran, only two hours ahead of them. They had been standing by the exit door, waiting for her to pick them up. Hearing that gave her goose bumps.

At last they checked into the hotel. In spite of its dreadful beginning, that summer of 1984 proved to be a welcome vacation. The four children were playful, as if no time had passed since they were young kids who used to play ball together in the large back yard of their grandma's home in Teheran.

Moosh, who was sixteen now, was the leader of the team. Her aunt was surprised that she had turned into such a well-behaved young lady. Roy was the same age as his first cousin, almost fourteen. They both had thin black hair above their upper lips now and their voices had changed to a low pitch. The youngest was her sister's second son, who was seven. He had been crawling when they left. The sisters rejoiced in their reunion, six long years melted away in the warmth of their laughter.

In the meantime, she called Nigeria and reached her husband at the university. When she finally got John on the phone, he was desperately worried. "Why did it take you such a long time to call?" She told him a harmless version of their holdup in London, that the connecting flight to Austria had been delayed for two days.

He was glad to hear from them, but had bad news from Enugu. He didn't say much. "Look don't disturb your vacation with your sister, I'll call you back." He hung up in a rush before she could ask any questions.

While helping her sister rent a flat, she found time to visit her boss at her old work place. Everything was the same. Fewer employees, no new faces. They seemed to have survived the recession somehow. By the end of July she had registered Shana's boys at the nearest school.

Shana had transferred a large amount of money to Austria, and her husband was going to join her in a few months. They were planning to move to the United States. But as the US embassy in Iran was closed, they had come to Austria to get a visa from there. That was what most Persians had been doing since the revolution to be able to travel to most places in the world. The only foreign embassy with an office in Iran was Austria.

Everything was going so well. She was content, for she'd been able to help her sister and spare her the rough times she had gone through six years before. Now she felt she had completed her mission and was ready to go back to Enugu. Then her husband called. And with his phone call, her journey in life took another detour.

CHAPTER 18
Grim Under the Courtly Costume

"Rumor has it that the government is trying to limit public gatherings, as they could lead to anti-government movements. Especially in Enugu, because of the students. The Ibos have proven to be stubborn in the past." John told her when she called again.

"So what do you mean, I don't see the connection with us. What should we do?" Impatiently, she wanted to know more.

"The university might not open for next school year. Stay there. I'll stay here until September when the classes are supposed to open. If they don't, I'll leave too."

"I can't wait in Austria that long. Moosh and Roy have to go to school in September. I'll have to be back by then. Look, we'll stay until the end of July; maybe you'll know more by then." So he agreed, and wished her a good time with her sister.

Finally the time came, and she called her husband. He didn't have good news. "Things don't look good. No one has any idea if the university will open or not. You'd better not come back. If you're satisfied that the job market in Austria is the same as before, go to England."

"Well, that is more or less the case," she said abruptly to cut short the conversation. "And they won't let me enter the UK without you anyway."

She didn't want to accept that for the third time she was about to lose the home that she had secured for her children. Her new shelter. The nest that she had put together for her kids, like a bird, piece by piece.

But John convinced her that it was the right thing to do. He promised to take the first flight to England and be there before they arrived. At that moment she had a feeling that there was more to it than he admitted. He was aware of her attachment to Enugu, so happy she had been the past year, so he probably wasn't telling her the whole truth, not to unnerve her.

It was time to move on, she knew well, and couldn't escape the fact any more. Her destiny was being twisted. She was going to start again, in a country where the people had made the worst possible first impression on her.

When they reached the small lonely airport in Graz and said good-by to her sister, her heart was bleeding. Moosh and Roy didn't mind. As teenagers, they were pleased to hear that they were going back to live in Europe. Which was all right with her, at least she was spared their tears. And the rest was up to her anyway.

Because of what had happened to them in London she couldn't believe that she would be going back there within such a short time. She tried to comfort herself: "Maybe we were in the wrong place at the wrong time. Revolution and war are going on in Iran, and to the Europeans anyone with a Persian passport is either a spy or a terrorist."

Her logic made sense. But it didn't help her understand why each opportunity she found to live happily was taken away from her, so viciously. She innocently lost them over and over again.

Fortunately, this time they entered England smoothly, as John was waiting for them at the airport. They drove to Guildford, the little town where her in-laws lived, a half hour drive south of London. They were supposed to stay there until John could find out more.

While John was there, she could feel how embarrassed his parents made him feel, having married "someone from Iran," a Third World country, and a woman with two nearly grown kids. It wasn't hard to see it; her in-laws didn't hide their feelings. And then there was his brave, silent fight with them to justify himself, and make them accept his wife and the children.

This was her first confrontation with problems of cultural diversity in marriage. She felt sorry for him. On the other hand, she regretted for the first time having married a man of a different mentality. The intolerance of her in-laws hit her, in the most harsh and hurting way.

During the time she lived in England, the famous British "manners" proved to be perfect just for the English among themselves, not when they came across "the others." Because then, they turned into the only "worthy human beings" on the Earth. And as for the rest, they were weeds under an inch of manure. She encountered this attitude all during the six years, as she worked and mixed with all sorts of English citizens.

In the beginning, she took the first job she could find to get their life going in the meat department of a supermarket, mixing the minced meat in a bathtub with her bare hands. To get this job, she did not disclose her education and experience, fearing that she would seem overqualified for the position.

In time, she worked herself into an office job in the same supermarket in charge of scheduling for the whole five-hundred person staff. After that, she was promoted to do computerized payroll. Three years later, she left the supermarket to work as an account assistant in a credit card company, and later in a multi-million dollar insurance firm. During this time, she saw it all, both upper and lower levels of society. The degree of intelligence didn't seem to make any difference in an Englishman's attitude.

Her parents-in-law received them with outward kindness, yet not so pleased. Soon her husband left for Nigeria, leaving her and the children behind in his parents' house.

The in-laws were both in their seventies. John's father was a strange, prominent Scottish man, a living symbol of the English monarchy. He was a marine biologist and had received the second-highest medal of service to the country (OBE) during the Second

World War from King George II. He was on a pension now, but after the war, he had had a good position in the Food and Agriculture Organization (FAO) of the United Nation's headquarters in Italy.

His wife, a humble, introverted, vigorously active lady, was born in Innsbruck - Tyrol, West Austria, in the Alps. During the Second World War she had lived in the U.S., working as a governess for a privileged family. She had married the Englishman, an enemy, during the war in the Bahamas. They were an extremely complicated, secretive couple who had nothing in common what-so-ever with each other, or with their only son.

CHAPTER 19
Out of the Eighteen Years of Prison

The house that her in-laws lived in was called "The Steading." An enormous country-style home, more than a hundred years old. It was a two-story, 'L' shaped building with five bedrooms. The small front yard was accessible from the side road.

The road-side view of the house showed a rectangular brick wall up to the roof which made up the whole length of the house -- the long wing. It had two rows of small metal frame square windows, the glass of which was divided into smaller squares by metal strips. In front of the entrance door there was a narrow porch, a lamp hanging from the top.

The dining room expanded back into the garden, its door opposite the entrance of the house. The kitchen and staircase to the second floor were on the right. The house's best feature, as far as she was concerned, for she could enter the house, turn right, and go upstairs to their room without being noticed; other than the times that the in-laws were dining, when they let the door open to keep an eye on her activities. What struck her as odd was that there was a sink and tap water, cold and hot separate, in every bedroom. So they had to mix the water in the sink, and wash in standing water, which didn't appeal to her as hygienic.

The garden included acres of land, covered by what they called lawn, but looked more like a hundred years of weeds mowed carefully. An old, tall pine tree was standing right in the middle of the garden.

When John left, things got worse. His parents' coldness escalated into actual cruelty. She had never expected such a hideous attitude from people in a nation that is so well known for politeness and manners.

Yet, she always remained calm and quiet. She smiled, however humiliated, as they ridiculed her culture and religion. She took it submissively each time they reduced her proud existence to dirt, and every time she was at a loss to find answers to their purposely twisted and preconceived questions about the revolution, the Shah of Iran, and the Persian way of life.

In those difficult days what kept her from throwing herself out the window were her prayers and the children who needed her. Moosh and Roy didn't know what was going on. She kept them busy in the bedrooms upstairs, and as far away from the in-laws as possible.

She didn't have a penny. Because John hadn't been able to exchange money in Nigeria, he left her with only some Niara (Nigerian currency). And she soon discovered that no bank in England would honor or exchange them, as the Niara was not an internationally recognized currency.

By the end of August she still hadn't heard from John. She didn't know what to do, but her intuition told her to look for a school for the children. So she did, and on tenth of September when they were to start classes, there was still no sign of her husband.

Every morning she sent Moosh and Roy off and in the afternoon when they came back, she would take them upstairs quietly and stay with them in their bedrooms. She helped them do their homework, and made sure they didn't make much noise. They were extraordinarily cooperative. The bond between the three of them had grown so strong that they understood each other even without words.

Throughout their stay with the in-laws, and despite all the insults, she remained respectful and polite to them to show them how much she appreciated their help. Especially, as John had asked them to lend her money for the children's bus fare to school. That was the smallest she ever felt. But she had to swallow her pride.

It wasn't until November that she finally received a letter from

Nigeria. John had no hope that the Enugu University would open. He was coming back to England.

When he returned, he told her that he hadn't been allowed to transfer any money from Nigeria to England. Not even his last month's wages. They both were down to zero, from every point of view.

"Well," she said "We start again." And they went out looking for work. By Christmas of that year she and John were both employed, and on the seventh of January 1985, they could afford to throw a little birthday party for Moosh in a house they had rented.

The year Moosh turned seventeen, she graduated from high school. And in September, seven years after they had fled their country, she entered college. At the same time she took a part-time job at McDonald's to help with the family's finances.

The English education system is not like other European countries. There is no entrance exam to get a place in the university. After graduating from high school, if the students plan to go to university, they have to attend a two-year college. And this is only possible for them if they have exceptionally good grades. Only after finishing college can they apply to the university. At this step, acceptance depends purely on the grade point average of the two college years. That means, there is enormous competition, and only the students with the highest grades can hope to succeed.

While Moosh was in college, she showed a great interest in mathematics, so she planned to go on and study a math-related subject. During her two years in college, she proved to have the perseverance and will to succeed. She studied hard and her chances of entering a university looked great. Yet something peculiar was happening to Roy.

He was fifteen when he entered the English system, but the harder he tried the less successful he was in earning the grades he deserved. Strangely, when the school psychologist examined him, it was reported that there was nothing wrong with him. But neither Roy nor she were satisfied.

So, they looked for a professional outside the school. Several educational psychologists examined him. Roy's IQ was high, and they could find no other problem. His low grades at school, they said, were due to the language deficiency, as he now was trying to master a third language.

But his mother didn't accept the conclusion, so they were referred to a psychotherapist. His opinion was that Roy was fine, just very anxious, perhaps due to the childhood experiences with his father. Finally, one after another, all the experts concluded that maybe his low grades were due to his own lack of interest in studying.

Still, she was certain that something was wrong. She had worked with him and other children in Teheran, in Austria, Nigeria, and now in England. So, she was positive that Roy was not disinterested. Why all the specialists failed to identify the problem, she couldn't explain.

"Every mother thinks that her son is the best. You have to accept the fact that Roy is simply not a study-oriented person." She would not take that as an answer, even though everyone laughed at her.

Getting similar advice from various specialists disheartened the young Roy. He became depressed, more difficult to help, and finally he fulfilled their prophecies and actually lost interest. At this point he rebelled against school, studying, and his mother for "pointlessly pushing and punishing him," he used to say.

Roy turned fifteen in November 1985. He was to graduate the next year. But he had lost his self-confidence. The way it looked, he had no chance of going to college, and although he never refused his mother's help, he was obviously an unwilling student and argued constantly that it was a waste of time. But she had no intention of letting him give up so easily. Neither was she going to give up on him.

Time went by, and Christmas of 1985 brought good tidings. The first one was her in-laws change of heart. This happened when they finally realized that she was not "after" anything from their son, other than having a warm family life. And as they noticed that she and John were both working hard to achieve just that, they offered to help them make a down-payment on a house.

The second happy event was Moosh's eighteenth birthday on the seventh of January 1986. This was a distinctive moment in the life of a mother who had always lived for her children.

When she divorced her ex-husband, and got custody of Moosh and Roy, she continually lived in fear, a consequence of his merciless reaction to the divorce and the kidnapping of their son. And the fact that she had lied to him, taking the children to Austria, and never returning.

Over eleven years had passed since their divorce, and eight years since the day they left Iran. Throughout all these years she suffered from a deadly anxiety that her ex-husband might still attempt to take the children away from her. She was convinced that he was the kind of person who would do anything to hurt her. And because of his visitation rights, he could have easily claimed them through the Iranian embassy, and force them to return to Iran.

This horror followed her like a dark shadow, wherever she went and whatever she did. She often had dreadful dreams, night after night. Her former husband was knocking on the door, taking the kids away from her. She'd wake up terrified, thanking dear God each night, that it was only a dream.

So, she had always looked forward to this day, when her Moosh would turn eighteen, and her father would no longer have any claim on her.

The 7th of January 1986, was the day she was released from the prison inside her, which no one saw her in; that dreaded place where fear had been a cruel and constant jailer. And no one would know how it feels to live there for eighteen years.

CHAPTER 20
The Fourth Relapse

On an exceptionally beautiful day in February 1986, they moved into their own home, a joyous occasion for the whole family. It was not a big house, but it was their own. It had three spacious bedrooms upstairs, and a little square back yard that had received no attention from the previous owner. The kitchen window looked out on the front yard and the road, and an old unhealthy grapevine was just behind it.

Roy and Moosh had their own bedrooms, and immediately began decorating them. Moosh, who had an income now, bought herself a beautiful set of furniture: a four-door wardrobe, a dressing table, two bed-side stands, and curtains. The furniture was a bright, bluish color, with white strips around the corners. Her curtains were white, with modern patterns in light-blue and green. Everything matched the off-white color of the wall paper.

Roy's room was the smallest bedroom, but he was quite happy. She decorated his room. He didn't have any specific wishes, so she did the best she could.

Their time together was going from good to better and best. Moosh was studying diligently and planned to apply to Imperial College of London University to study computer science engineering. Roy was still getting extra tutoring at home.

She and John worked hard and earned a good income. John got a brand new company car, and they were entitled to choose any one they liked at the dealership. Everything seemed perfect.

A year went by and she was happier than ever before. She arranged their home with pictures of the family, memorial objects, and hand-made Persian tablecloths. Whatever happened outside the house was of little consequence; inside was a little Persia, and a true Persian family lived there.

Moosh and Roy, who had begun their teenage years in Nigeria, were continuously reminded by their mother how miserable their life would have been in Africa, if their black peers had not taken to them in such a warm-hearted manner. If they had treated them like enemies, just because they were different. Like many whites who did, those who isolated themselves in their "monarchy" treating the natives like servants.

Using live examples, she made them see the good in people as well as the bad. "You can learn from both. Follow the way of true human beings, and avoid to act like those who aren't." Persian words of wisdom.

In this case, she was asking them to behave somewhat differently from almost everyone else in Europe. So she often had to argue and prove that most of those around them were wrong, that the youngsters who lived a "wild life" were not doing things the right way. To her, it was a solo fight against the majority of Europe's younger generation, not an easy task by any means.

But she did it, by constantly making her children notice the consequences of the so-called "wild life," such as teen pregnancies, school drop-outs, and the lower level of life resulting from a lack of education.

There were sufficient examples in the stories they heard together in the news every day, as well as the statistics which showed Europe's high rate of suicide and divorce. She made them aware of the miserable life led by addicted youngsters who were drawn in by their fascination with what they called "freedom" and a search for "fun."

So, in 1987 when Moosh turned nineteen, the principles of morality and decency were already well ingrained. She had grown into a wise, and extremely independent young girl. She benefitted from the vast possibilities available to her, living in a European country, combined with a deep respect for her Persian roots.

In May of that year, she finished college and was accepted by the university of her first choice. She was leaving home to live in London, at the university's dormitory. It was an extraordinary accomplishment for Moosh, having been schooled in England for only three years, after learning English in Nigeria just a year before that. Moosh's achievement gave Mom a sense of fulfillment too; she was one step nearer to one of her own goals.

The day Moosh left, they both cried bittersweet tears of joy and sorrow. She held her daughter in her arms, and whispered the last words of advice, *"I have no hesitation about letting you go, dearest, for I know that you are a wise girl. There is only one thing I need to ask of you. I am perfectly aware that you appreciate my sacrifices that got you here. Yet don't ever feel the need to be sorry for me; you don't owe me anything, and don't you ever make a decision in your personal life for my sake, to make me happy, as I did for my mother. Be careful not to make the same mistake I did."*

"The only thing you can do for me, to show your gratitude, is to take good care of yourself, for I won't be there to do it for you. This is my dearest wish and the only thing I beg you to do for your mother. It will give me peace of mind, for you and Roy are more important to me than anything else in the world."

After Moosh left, Roy was lost and lonely. The house felt empty without her. Mom didn't go into Moosh's empty bedroom for months. To her it was as if the house had lost its balance, it was lighter, it sloped on that side where Moosh used to live. But one month later a fortunate event came to their rescue. Her youngest sister called from Teheran to say that they would soon be leaving Iran, and going to the United States. They needed a formal invitation from her and an affidavit of support, in order to get a tourist visa for

England, which was the condition set by the UK embassy in Iran. From there they'd go to California. She sent the papers immediately.

The events that caused a total breakdown in the relationship between Persia and the United States began on November the 4th, 1979 during Jimmy Carter's presidency. The day the Iranian revolutionary guard took over the U.S. embassy in Teheran and took all American employees hostage.

In 1980, when U.S. government's attempt to rescue the hostages failed, the situation became even worse. It was absolutely impossible for Persians to travel to the United States until January 1981, the day of President Reagan's inauguration. That same day the hostages were released and the siege ended.

During Mr. Reagan's administration, although the relationship between the two countries remained strained, many doors opened to Persians to travel to the U.S., or even apply for political asylum. But the U.S. embassy in Teheran remained closed, and Iranians who wished to enter the U.S. had to go to another country and obtain a visa from there.

Around that time her sister, Shana, whose husband had joined her in Austria, managed to get visas there. She and her family were now living in San Diego, California. Nearly every family with young boys and financial possibilities, was trying to flee from Iran. The risk of their young children being taken to the front was such a strong threat that they chose any country where they had a relative or a friend, and fled their homeland.

A large number of families collapsed after they left; their children fell into the wrong hands or they suffered financial ruin. Many of them got caught while trying to escape, on foot or hiding under a car; and were executed.

At the time she received the news of her youngest sister, her brother was also in Iran planning to get out. But their mother had no intention of leaving. She was emotionally bound to the house where her children had grown up and her husband had died.

"I wish to die in my home, even If I have to be buried under the Iraqi's bombs," she stubbornly insisted.

Most of the older generation felt as she did and stayed in their homes, and many of them actually did die as a result. It was a disastrous ending for one of the richest cultures in the world -- the once so enormous and powerful kingdom of Persia.

Finally the time came for her sister to arrive at the London airport with her two children. Her husband had remained in Teheran, to make sure that his family got out safely, and he was planning to join them later. It had often happened that passengers were turned away at the airport, and told later that they were not allowed to travel (with or without reason). In those days, nobody could be certain of safe passage until the last minute when they stepped into the aircraft.

And so nine years after that fateful summer day in Tehran 1978, when she packed her suitcases and said good-bye, when everything was as it always had been since they remembered, she saw her sister again. Her sister had only one baby then, and she was in the hospital with her as she gave birth. Now, it was another summer 1987, and she was there with a girl of ten, and a little boy who had never seen his aunt.

Apart from the joy of their reunion, having her sister out of danger was a heavy weight off her shoulders. All through those years away from home, the thought of her troubled family in Iran had over-shadowed her few happy moments. Now that both her sisters were free and safe, her happiness was more complete than ever before. She always thought she didn't know her youngest sister so well. Since she married and left Teheran, they had only seen each other on occasions. But when they met, they knew each other too well. The distance had not effected their feelings for each other a little bit.

Her sister was going to stay with them until she heard from her husband. When he was out of Iran, they would go to the U.S. together. It took over two months. By the time her husband managed to come out, her poor sister was thoroughly distraught. She went through a nerve racking time. After having survived the revolution and that barbaric war for seven years, this was too much for her delicate nerves. She looked older than her age, and had lost a lot of her black hair. But she still was taking it bravely and never showed the slightest sign of weakness, for her children's sake. She was on the verge of a breakdown when her husband finally called.

Fortunately, everything went well from then on. She helped her sister to get a visa at the U.S. embassy in London, and a month later they left England to live with Shana until they settled in.

One year later in 1988, the Iran-Iraq war ended. Her brother then left the country through Germany and joined his two sisters.

Life kept getting better for the entire family now. Moosh was doing well at university. And Roy graduated with a desire to follow her. In the summer of that year they even had enough savings to take an exciting vacation on one of the most beautiful beaches of south England and celebrate the happy events. That was their first real vacation since they had left home. The four of them headed to the seaside, and spent quality time together in an exquisite holiday resort.

When they returned, another piece of good news was waiting for them -- the most exciting of all. It was a letter for Moosh, from the U.S. embassy in London. The year before, Shana had called from San Diego and told them of a visa lottery that was being held by the U.S. immigration office each year. That year, Shana said, Persians born outside Iran could apply and having been born in Germany, Moosh was entitled.

Although it was too far-fetched to think that she might win, Moosh filled out the forms and sent them away. Until that day, a year later, they had forgotten all about it. The letter she received from the embassy said that Moosh had actually won the lottery and could submit her papers and receive an immigration visa for the U.S.

In the summer of 1990, when Moosh graduated from the

university and received her computer-engineering degree, she left England for San Diego.

The only dark corner of their life at this point was Roy's learning difficulty. He had graduated from high school, but because of his low grades, none of the colleges had accepted him. And all their attempts to find a way had failed.

Ultimately she thought of meeting with the school's principal, and asking for his help. Maybe Roy could be given a second chance; maybe they would let him retake the last school year. It was not unusual, but it was entirely up to the principal's discretion. Roy was eager to do it, but he was not ready to ask anyone for a favor.

When she arrived at the school she explained to the principal that Roy's IQ was well above average.

"I am certain that Roy's low grades are not because he is too lazy to study as you've stated. He is, in fact, very disappointed not to have been able to enter college."

The principal was barely listening. She tried to convince him, "You see, every member of my family is a university graduate; his problem cannot be a matter of attitude, so please help him."

Before she finished her last sentence, as if the principal's ego was affected, he looked down his English nose at her and interrupted: "Well, not everyone has to go to university. This country needs carpenters and cleaners too. You have to accept that your son is not an intellectual, even if *all your family* is educated," he emphasized the last part of his speech so painfully sarcastic, she felt like crying.

"Send him off to learn something else. Maybe he'll become a good factory worker, or machine operator. In my opinion you are fooling yourself." He went on, moving in his chair to let her know that the meeting was over.

That day she came out of his office angry, insulted and disappointed. Something inside kept telling her all the way that the principal was wrong. But he wouldn't believe her, nor did anyone. The last door seemed to have closed on Roy.

At this point, Roy settled for a course in the insurance brokering field. He found a place at the famous Lloyds of London, and enrolled for the training course. Yet they were both unhappy. Until one day, two years later as Roy was nearing the end of his course, things suddenly changed.

One Sunday evening she was home, watching TV; a program about youngsters' achievements. They were talking with a young man who had obtained a university degree, despite learning difficulties he had. As the young man explained the details of his problems, she noticed similarities to Roy's. That young man, they said, had a condition called dyslexia. The next day she was on the phone to the TV station, asking for more information.

She found out that dyslexia was a learning disorder, not yet well-known in England. Very few specialists were able to diagnose it at the time, and there were no special programs in the education system for students with this disability.

So she searched the entire country. A month later she found an educational psychologist in a remote village north of London who specialized in dyslexia, and took Roy to see him.

The specialist performed two tests on Roy, each of which took the better part of a day. At the end, he confirmed her suspicion; Roy did indeed suffer from dyslexia.

Dyslexia, which remains undetected in many children even now, is a condition that can only be diagnosed by a special educational psychologist. Among the first symptoms, which appeared in Roy's early childhood, was an inability to learn, tell and feel the time dimension; directions (right, left, up, down) and confusion when following more than one order at a time. Later in life, dyslexic children, will have difficulty reading, remembering, writing, and expressing themselves. The latter causes frustration, anger, and tendency to become introverted. Almost always they are misunderstood. And finally, when they don't do well at school, most of them simply give up.

When the news reached Moosh in San Diego, she called

immediately, "Dyslexia is a well-known condition in the United States. There is help and accommodation available for such students. If you send Roy to me I'll help him, and he *can* enter college." What a relief! Although it came after Roy had wasted two years of his life, because those so-called professionals didn't listen and didn't care.

It was 1990, and by then Roy was twenty years old. That summer he completed his course, and she sent him to California. He stayed with Shana, and enrolled at Mesa College in San Diego in September of that year. He graduated from the Criminal Justice Department of San Diego State University in 1997 and was accepted by the law schools of three universities the same year he graduated. In his entry essay he wrote, "I want to study law, because I know how it feels to experience injustice. I like to help the helpless people, like myself in England, and my mother as she was twenty seven years ago, to receive justice."

But all that, didn't come easy. Just as Roy finished his first semester in Mesa College, his mother's life suffered another disturbing blow. This time, it hit her worse than ever.

By the end of eighties, the recession that took over Europe while they were in Austria gradually hit the United Kingdom. When John Major defeated Margaret Thatcher, and became prime minister of the United Kingdom, people's hopes rose.

Strangely enough, the new young prime minister had the same learning disorder as Roy. He had dyslexia, and for the same reason he had dropped out from university. The prime minister had no degree. He had worked his way up to his country's highest office through his political abilities and intelligence alone. John Major managed to keep the country from going under, but recovery was long in coming. Interest rates went up and unemployment rose. There are no fixed-rate home loans in England, so mortgage payments increased along with the interest rates for home owners. This made hundreds of families lose their homes, as well as their jobs.

This happened at the time when Roy had successfully completed his first semester at Mesa College and Moosh was working in San Diego. She, too, had taken minimum-wage jobs initially; gone bravely through the hardship of being far from her family in a new continent where she bicycled to work at the beginning.

She then had moved on working in a bank. And as a computer engineer, she had no difficulty finding a good job soon after. Now she had her own car and lived in a rented apartment. But Roy needed support to survive and study. As a foreign student, he had to pay full tuition fees, and that was expensive.

As is usually the case, the building industry was hit first. John's company went bankrupt, and he lost his job. Just as she had found a way for Roy to continue his education, she found herself with no funds to support him.

Her income alone was not enough for everything: Roy's education, an increasingly high mortgage, and everyday expenses. She was devastated. The thought of Roy losing this God-send chance to study was killing her. Her mind was everywhere, but didn't get anywhere, and the more she searched for a way to make it work, the more helpless and lost she became.

She was tired. After twenty-four years of running fast, since she first got married, now at forty-four years of age, she didn't have the stamina to return to the starting gate. Still, as unfair as it was to her, the only solution seemed to be to sell their house, for time was running out and she was not going to let Roy down.

Soon after she came to this painful conclusion, her mind spiraled out of control. The sleeping memories of the past awoke; the challenges she had mastered had sapped her energy and finally caused her to break.

She blamed it on her ex-husband who had never paid a dime for their children. Never even made an attempt to get in touch or write a letter. She hated him more than ever, now that Roy's future was at stake. The negative power of this hate and hostility that she allowed herself to feel for the first time in her life, soon consumed her to the bitter end.

When she was awake, she constantly saw her daughter's innocent face talking to her: "Mom, I miss you here. Mom, my boyfriends laugh at me when I tell them I'm a virgin. They say something must be wrong with me. Mom, why do we have to be different from everyone else? How do you know that your way of raising us is the correct way, while the majority of girls don't believe in my kind of virtues? Mom, I miss you. I need your moral support."

And she saw her son's desperate face, asking her, "Mom, why did you give me such a hard time and make me study all those extra hours? Well, you could not have known that I was dyslexic, but I didn't deserve that humiliation. Why did you make me go away, while I'm still not sure if I can make it or not ? Why? . . . why? . . . why?"

She always believed in what she did, raising her children. She was aware that Roy had lost his self-confidence when he was thrown out of school. But she had never lost faith in him. Yet in those moments, her mind was working against her, driving her into destructive self-doubt. The pressure and the pain were taking over, making her feel guilty for everything that had gone wrong in her life.

When she slept she was tormented by dreams. All the anguish she had pushed to the back of her mind, so she could go on, now reappeared coming back like phantoms. She saw herself lost in the forest with her baby Moosh, and foxes were tearing them apart. Sometimes she was in the Austrian castle. Ghosts with faces like the judge in the divorce court, were haunting her ready to snatch away her children. Then, they were on death row in the immigration jail, and officers who looked like angels of death were coming to take them away.

It went on like this, until one night when she underwent a peculiar experience. It was not a dream.

That night she was in bed upstairs and her husband was watching TV down in the living room. As her eyes warmed up, she saw a mass, a radiant nebulous globe. It entered the bedroom, from the open window by the foot of her bed. It glided across the room above her body, spinning gently. It passed by her, then disappeared as it reached the wall above her head.

She fell asleep before she could wonder what it was. Some time later she felt a presence in the bedroom. Thinking it was her husband coming to bed, she turned over, pulled the blanket up to her chin, and tried to go back to sleep. Moments later, she felt her blanket being gently pulled away, from the foot of the bed, as if he were teasing her. "Leave me alone," she protested and pulled up the blanket. It happened a second time, and then a third time.

She eventually lost her temper, sat up and scolded him. "John, I said leave me alone. I'm not in the mood for jokes." But she got no answer. She looked around, but didn't see anyone. *Maybe he is hiding*, she thought. So she didn't make much of it. She put her head down on the pillow and fell into a dreamless sleep.

When she woke the next morning, she felt somehow different. It was a Sunday morning. She went down and found her husband in the living room. "Why did you do that last night?" she asked him angrily. "You know if you wake me up in the middle of the night, I can't go back to sleep so easily."

He looked at her baffled, "I didn't do anything to you last night," he said. "I fell asleep on the couch last night, watching a movie."

She gazed at him suspiciously. "Didn't you pull the blanket off me? And after I told you not to do that for the third time, didn't you lift me off the bed with both your hands?"

"What are you talking about?"

"I am not stupid. You held me, with your hands underneath my back for a while, didn't you? Then you kissed me on the forehead, and put me down."

Concerned he kept repeating, "No I didn't," looking at her mesmerized, thinking, *I hope she isn't losing her mind*. But he didn't say anything more.

When she saw the look on his face, she let herself fall on the couch. "Then it was my father. I thought it was you," she said looking melancholy. "It was him. He came again, to give me a lift in life, and in a way, I think he did."

She couldn't explain her experience, but what happened soon

after made her believe that she was right. Her father had saved her once again, from falling over the edge into deadly darkness.

Unbelievably, after that night she regained her peace of mind and her lost strength and hope. The painful decision of selling the house and losing her little sanctuary to raise funds for Roy's education didn't bother her any more. From that night on nothing frightened her anymore, even when *she* ultimately lost her job, too.

The sale didn't go smoothly, for there were hundreds of repossessed houses on the market at a rock-bottom price. Their house stayed on the market for a whole year, and as a result Roy lost two semesters at college. But finally they found a buyer.

On the day they moved out, her heart was broken. Each time she tore up her roots, it was hard. But leaving her first owned home made it that harder for her to let go, more than each time before. She was in mid-life now, and had to start anew. Once again, for the fifth time.

She had no regrets, but for years she missed her home, and she cried each time she remembered a corner, a piece, or a cherished moment from that happy time. The garden she had created from the wasteland of a back yard was so beautiful that every prospective buyer had complimented her on it. The grapevine behind the kitchen window that she had cultivated, had grown to cover the old wood panels on the front porch. Now there were bunches of grapes hanging, just in front of the entrance every summer.

Most of the houses in England have names, and she loved that tree so much that she called the house *The Vine*. While they were waiting for a buyer, she painted over the house number, and put the name sign up. The house was number thirteen. For her, it was lucky, but she was sure that some didn't buy it on that basis alone. But strangely enough, the man who bought it did so primarily because thirteen was his lucky number too. Was that all accidental?

They moved back to her in-laws, where she had started. The same old story. There she was certain that if she was to start over once more, she would not do it without her children. Now, with Roy and Moosh gone, she had no reason to stay in England.

She made John apply for a student visa at the University of

California, where he could get his Ph.D., and he left for San Diego in the summer of 1992. She was still hanging on to a temporary job to meet the expenses. In October she quit, a proud feeling; when everyone was looking for work! Then she bought a ticket, and left England to join her children in the "dream land."

Sitting in the DC-10, flying to the unknown, she was taking with her three important dreams: To build another home for her children; to see her Moosh marry happily, and present her with grandchildren; and to attend Roy's graduation.

Since the children had left, she had lived for these dreams. Night after night, she had closed her eyes and envisioned: A beautiful house, her daughter in a wedding dress, waving her good-bye from a limousine, and Roy as a lawyer, in a dark suit and tie, a briefcase in hand, on his way to court.

High in the cloudless sky she was only thinking of the future. *If I could make it in Persia, Germany, Austria, Africa, and England, I can make it in San Diego.* And someone was singing a song about New York.

"Start spreading the news, I'm leaving today
I want to be a part of it - New York, New York
If I can make it there, I'll make it anywhere
It's up to you - New York, New York"

She remembered how much she liked that handsome young singer when she was a teenager. And never, even in her wildest dreams could she imagine one day living in the same country as Frank Sinatra. She never imagined that she would even be there to hear of his massive heart attack and people who'd say, "I don't think he's gonna make it this time."

When the captain announced they were preparing to land in San Diego, she looked out the window. It was the most beautiful sunny

October day she had ever experienced. Nothing like the freezing, foggy morning when she took a taxi to the airport in London.

And when she arrived in San Diego, she found herself back home. The reunion was one of the happiest moments of her life since she had left Persia fourteen years back. Each of the four siblings was the head of a family of four, and her mother was also there for a visit, so that made seventeen of them. This coastal city, just a few miles north of Mexico, was like a tiny piece of Teheran, a small Persia. She felt she was home.

The song was still going through her mind: *"It's up to you, New York, New York."*

PART VII
END OF THE JOURNEY IN SAN DIEGO, A TOWN BY THE SEA

CHAPTER 21
I Handed Over My Life Achievement to Strangers

The phone hasn't stopped ringing all day. I haven't taken calls for two days, haven't even checked my messages. The calendar on the desk says it is 1997. A Saturday, early afternoon. I have to finish what I started, because I'll be flying to Oklahoma one of these days. My son and me; it sounds great.

I run one more spell-check, almost done. Put the arrow on "print" and click on "print all pages" and wait.

Ouch, a message appears on the screen. It says: *Error. Printer not ready. 'Retry' or press 'Help'.* I check the printer. It's not on. No wonder it's not ready. I turn it on, and press 'Retry.' When it starts making scraping noises, it tells me that it is printing.

So, I sit back waiting for it to finish, and look out, thinking. This time there was no need to click on and get help instantly. I wish it were just like that in real life. So easy and available, whenever help is needed.

"I need some help soon, I have to fly again!" I tell the computer without looking at it. No response for my kind of need!

At a certain point in my past, I don't know when, I developed vertigo and fear of flying. It is strange, after having spent so many hours in the air in and out of so many countries. Well, anyway this is not going to stop me from flying to Oklahoma. Especially now that I strongly feel that my son needs me to be with him. One of the rare occasions, that even he says so.

He is twenty-seven, leaving for Oklahoma to study law at Tulsa University. I am so proud of him, and he knows it. We are both excited and confused. This time he probably won't come home again, except for visits. He'll get married and build his own nest for his wife and children.

I miss him already, but I'm trying not to convey my frailty. I want him to feel free, and to fly as high as he wishes to without worrying about me. I know he can, I have raised him this way. His wings are strong enough, and he is tough enough to survive. All he needs now is my moral support.

It is so quiet here. The printer has stopped. The interruption of its rhythmic scratching sound takes me out of my thoughts. But I continue looking outside. Funny, for the last six months I have been sitting on this chair, on and off for hours looking out the window and writing, but haven't really noticed this fine picture. The beauty of the garden I have created here.

Home -- what a holy place. It strikes me that some say, "Home is where your heart is." I don't know if they have ever faced losing their homeland, so it's easy for them to say so. I think your heart is where your home is. My home was taken away from me twenty years ago. It probably doesn't even exist anymore, not the way I knew it. But I have re-created it wherever destiny has taken me, in many places of the world, for however short a time. I have loved each one, and felt safe and serene in all of them. But still, my heart is far away. Where I started.

I hear the phone ring again. My husband doesn't take the calls. He says, "They're all for you anyway, your family." I don't think he is home at the moment. He must have gone to Home Depot to buy hardware; he is doing some repairs around the house.

He really is not a handyman. John is an intellectual, but he doesn't mind doing small projects in the house, mostly for me. Because he knows if he doesn't, I'll do it myself and then he'll have to help me. This makes things more difficult for him, for he knows "what I start," I'll finish as perfectly as possible. My perfectionism always puts him in trouble. So, to avoid that, he tries his best to take care of these tasks before I jump in and make more work for both of us.

Tomorrow is Sunday, so I'll have the day to rest, and on Monday I'll see my babies. It is so wonderful seeing them every morning. They are not really mine; I just take care of them for their mothers. But this is only metaphysically spoken, in my heart they are mine and will always be.

It's so strange, my friends often ask me if taking care of babies is hard work, and too much responsibility. I agree to the latter, but hard work -- no. Is there *anything* like an easy job in the world? The point is, as they say, if we love what we do, it's easy to work hard.

When I gave birth to my children, this infinite pool of love came into my heart. It is still full. This love needs to be given away, otherwise I might explode. And my "babies" are receiving it now. Now, that I have handed over my own children to strangers. My own children! Wrong expression. They no longer belong to "only me." Yet they are my greatest achievement, for which I have sacrificed thirty years of my life. Two healthy and successful members of society.

I worked hard to get them where they are now, and enjoyed every moment of it. I remember the days when we played in the park together, when the three of us learned to swim in the deep part of the pool at the same time! As I was teaching them to walk, to talk, to dance and sing. The long days it took me to teach them to ride their bicycles, and then to drive.

I have received so many compliments about them, and each one is as if a medal pinned on my chest.

But now, it's getting late, and I have to move on. I clear my desk and go downstairs to check the messages on the answering machine.

The first one is my brother, inviting us for his son's birthday. His daughter graduated this year. His son is still in high school. They are both wonderful children. They all live in Coronado, a forty-five minute drive from us.

The next message is from my daughter. She doesn't say much. Then my youngest sister; she just wants to see how I am doing. And why I am in hiding again. They live near us, and her son, too, graduated this year; her daughter, the little baby I still remember her as, is at university. She is planning to study a medicine-related subject, and my mother is very proud of her, because she is choosing a career that has been in the family for generations, starting with my grandfather, then my father, and all his brothers.

The next call is my daughter again. She says she'll call back. And then my son-in-law. His messages always make me laugh. He says: "Halo, it's me, your most favorite son in-law." (I have only one!) He goes on: "I know you are there listening, pick up the phone. Aha, you are laughing. Because you are there, but just don't want to pick up. That's all right. I'll try later."

He is such a loving young man. He keeps reminding me to mention him in my book. But I only did it because he truly is a wonderful man, and takes a good care of my Moosh. What I most like about him is that he is a believer, a true believer, and this has made him a good human being.

The next message is another one from my daughter. She says: "Halo, Mom, its me, Moosh. Haaaaaaalo. Halo. Haloooooo." She always does this. Long "halos," to give me time to pick up the phone if I am around. "Okay, Mom," she says, "If you don't call me by this evening, I'll have to come and check on you. Mo... om, pick up the phoooone. What is going on? Give me a call."

Oh, I think, *how much I love this creature.* Then the machine cuts itself off; she has used up the time allowed for one message. And no more.

I turn around and look at her wedding picture on the fireplace. And remember how hard it was the day she said good-bye and vanished from my life in a white limousine that said *Just Married* on the back. Isn't it amazing? I used to go to church day after day, and pray asking the Holy Mother to bring my daughter to her senses, to let her get married and settled down. I knew she was scared of marriage. The memories of her father, and what he did to me caused her to be wary. That day my prayers were finally heard, and soon she was off on her honeymoon. But there I was, standing on the pavement, crying, long after the car had disappeared. Letting her go was the hardest part of motherhood for me -- my final and most difficult task.

I move on to the other pictures on the wall. My Roy's graduation, when he got his BS degree. I remember that day; there were three thousand mothers at San Diego State University watching just like me. Moosh and her husband were also there, and she captured those magical moments on film. I'm glad she did because as soon as Roy walked on the stage to receive his degree, I was blinded by tears and my whole body started to shake. And every picture I took was blurred.

John and Moosh were also crying. "Mom, you did it. It was a long way, but you made it. You did it, Mom," she kept saying. It really didn't matter to me. "He did it," I said. "He did it himself." What mattered to me was that it was Roy up there on the stage, turning another one of my dreams into reality. All I had to say was: *Thank you, God.*

Finally, on theopposite wall, an old family photo catches my eye. It is from forty years ago, all six of us. I look at my father's face. "Hi, Dad, I did it, rest easy. Thanks for all your help." He is looking at me with that unique one- sided smile of his.

I still sometimes feel his presence, thirty years after he left us.

And my mother, she is in Teheran now, in the house of my memories. It is now nineteen years since I left Teheran, and I haven't been back yet. Everyone keeps telling me, "Don't go there, it is not like before. Keep your memories alive."

Now that all four of us are here in San Diego, with families, my mother lives a few months in Teheran and then a few months here with one of us.

Two sharp knocks on the door make me jump. It is almost nine in the evening. Who can that be? Before I open the door, Moosh walks in. She has a key to the house. She knows, for her, this house will always remain her home.

"Mom, why aren't you answering your messages? You worried me," she tells me off!! "I had to come and check on you. Can you tell me what's going on?"

I give her a big hug and say "Nothing is wrong, I was just finishing my memoir. I didn't want to fly to Oklahoma with Roy and worry about my book all the time. Come in. Sit yourself down."

She calms down and takes a seat on the couch. "Are you worried about him?"

I don't answer, just look at her. Her long black curly hair is flowing down her shoulders. In my eyes, she is still the pretty little four-year old who used to sit for me for hours while I put her long hair in ponytails. And cried my head off each time I decided to cut them short.

I glance at her body curiously and ask myself, *Is she? She is not! Or it doesn't show yet. Maybe next month.*

And then I see her, as in my latest dream, giving birth to *her* baby. Oh, how long I have dreamed of this wondrous moment. And now it has come so much closer. Sometime in the near future, another Moosh, or Roy is going to be born; for me to love, I know it. And then I remember a bumper sticker I once read on the back of a car: "The universe rearranges itself to accommodate your reality." One can only hope so.

Printed in the United States
28693LVS00001B/580-594